CW00819347

A PIPER'S TALE

STORIES FROM THE WORLD'S TOP PIPERS

Fergus Muirhead

WILLIAM GRANT & SONS

INDEPENDENT FAMILY DISTILLERS SINCE 1887

A Piper's Tale
978-1-908885-86-9
Fergus Muirhead
First Published 2013
Published by Cargo Publishing
SC376700
© Fergus Muirhead 2013

Printed & Bound in England by Martins
Cover design by Levente Szasbo
www.cargopublishing.com

Also available as:

Kindle Ebook
EPUB Ebook

For more, enjoy apiperstale.com

For Jane and Max

Foreword by Eddi Reader

When I was growing up in Glasgow, nobody in my family, as far as I was aware, was connected with Highland culture in a musical sense, although they taught me lots about the popular songs of the time. There was a real singing culture though, and each of us would take turns to sing at parties, especially at my Grandad Dan's house in Ruchill. As far as I was aware no one in the family played an instrument, although my Grandad said he remembered his relations playing the dulcimer, and he bought me one from Curlers Bar in the seventies when he noticed I was interested in learning music.

When I started doing some genealogy I realised that my great great great grandfather, Karl Rader, came to Scotland from Bavaria where he fought in the Scots colonies. I discovered that he is listed in the 1850 census as a street musician, and had been busking in Edinburgh. You can imagine my joy to discover he was a professional musician, making dulcimers and banjos. He had thirteen children and the eldest, James, came to Glasgow with his younger brother Daniel around 1870 and changed their names to Reader. Both married women with music hall connections (Daniel married the daughter of a blind violin playing Glasgow street musician) and I imagine they both repaired musical instruments as taught by their Prussian father.

James 'Jake' Rader, my great great grandfather, was an iron turner in Glasgow's Gallowgate. He had a son, Charles, who worked with John MacLean and who sung Robert Burns songs at Lodges all over Scotland. He was also involved with the Irish Foresters. Charles was father to my Great Uncles James and Alex, my Great Aunt Tizzy, who died in her twenties, and my Grandfather Dan.

Great Uncle James was the oldest and he learned to play the pipes in Glasgow. He had decided to write a book about the music and politics that he was involved in and I found all his manuscripts after I had to clear the Dublin home of his only son, who died aged eighty-seven. Everything was in the house and under the boiler in the shed, including two sets of moth-eaten pipes. It was all for the skip if I didn't take it home to Glasgow.

In his manuscript, he talks of a Glasgow that was full of pipe bands who marched up and down the streets playing Irish and Scottish music. They were school bands and Boys' Brigade bands, and in the early 1900s James talks about running barefoot through Glasgow with hundreds of people following pipe bands and enjoying the music. He educated himself and determinedly paid for lessons because he was keen to learn and in turn teach the Scouts that he was involved with.

He went to Ireland with the Scouts. Countess Markievicz was setting up relief funds for the poor in Dublin and she wanted the Scouts in Glasgow to collect for them, so they sent my Uncle James over as he was the Scout leader, even though he was only fifteen at the time. He went with his pipes, and Markievicz, James Connelly, and others involved in the revolution that was to take place a few years later, all begged him to go back to Glasgow and collect some old pipes so that they could set up their own band over there. They were keen that the musical link that had been established between Scotland and Ireland should be maintained.

Finding a piping family member who taught others helped me understand the validity of finding your culture through music because it showed me how his learning of the pipes made him feel connected to his community. He died in 1969, I only met him once, but now I feel that I have a closer relationship with him than with other family members who are still alive, and the reason for that is the musical connection and the pipes.

I used to love the sound of pipe bands, the sound of that skirling beautiful music, and it was live, not coming out of a box speaker. It was real and live and it encompassed your whole aural capacity, it got right into your marrow. That really fired me up as a musician, which I was when I first heard the bands in Glasgow because by then I was singing with my pals, forming wee bands and playing in the pubs. I met good people when we moved to Irvine and started going to folk clubs. Eleanor Shaw took me to Irvine Folk Club for the first time and I heard Heather Heywood singing. She blew my mind. She stood and sang an unaccompanied song, 'The Blacksmith', I think, and I realised you could sing in your own accent. I found a culture in folk clubs that was affiliated with Irish and Scottish music. I saw Archie Fisher and Christy Moore in Inverness and loved it all.

From the early days of hearing the pipes, and every time I hear them since, there is a sense of physical anatomical change in my body. I don't know what it is but I'd love to be able to make that sound, I'd love to be able to understand it more, and as far as all of the tunes are concerned, I find it quite romantic, but not in a fake sense; in an absolutely loving sense. When you hear a piper play on a street in Paris or Berlin or wherever, even a daft wonky drunk in Edinburgh, there is something incredibly familial about it and there is solidarity in the music that links me with my DNA. My DNA is a mixture of English, Irish, Scottish and Prussian, but I do know that I lean to Scotland. My background is here, my family is here, and when I hear the pipes I feel connected with who I am. I feel that I am owned by it as much as I own it, and when I feel like that I it's like I am a five-year-old again, being nurtured in the midst of my family. That's what the sound of it represents to me.

Foreword by Carlos Nuñez

The same year that I started to play Gaita, I saw the Royal Scots playing in front of my home, during the Celtic festival of Vigo. At the same time Galician folk band Milladoiro started to play Highland pipes, so many people discovered the instrument in Galicia then, but without a proper Scottish technique.

When I was thirteen I went for the first time to Lorient Festival to play the Gaita with a Symphony Orchestra and I met pipers such as Fred Morrison. Then, when I was sixteen, I decided to go to Brittany to study Highland pipes in the Conservatory of Ploemeur with Jean Luc Le Moign and Patrick Molard. I was interested not just in the technique but also about the writing system and the way of teaching, which I thought was also valid in many ways for the Gaita.

When I came back to Galicia I was so happy with everything I learned from Scottish, Irish and Breton pipers that Anton Corral, one of my Galician teachers, suggested that I bring some Highland pipe teachers to the Universidade Popular de Vigo to show all that knowledge to the rest of Galician pipers. It was amazing, and the best Gaita maestros of that time like Ricardo Portela and Milladoiro´s pipers came to the lessons. Everyone wanted to learn Scottish pipes.

At that time, in Galicia, the ornamentation was mostly orally transmitted and rarely written down, or it was written in a personal way, rather imprecise and poor. You might say this was good because it was less standardised, more alive if you will, but what actually happened is that ornamentation was being simplified and all the richness that the old pipers had in their playing was being lost. Listening to old recordings and a few old pipers, I realised they were playing most of the ornaments I had learnt from Scottish and Irish piping, but nobody was noticing. I started writing down very carefully all that wealth of knowledge, every piper would play different ones. Adding them up, it was quite an amazing complexity that I couldn't have imagined existed.

When, at eighteen, I passed the public examinations and became pipe professor at the Classical Conservatory in Vigo, I decided to design a system for writing the ornamentation based on the Scottish system, but using quavers and semiquavers also. I wanted to represent the gracenotes as closed, open and very open, the same with passing notes, flourishings, crossing noises, rubato, alternate open and close fingering; all those subtle ornamentations used by soloists and so characteristic of the bagpipes.

This new system was very well received, especially taking into account that my country is famous for being individualistic and having an anarchic spirit.

When I had been teaching for three years at the Conservatory I proposed to my colleagues from the Galician Pipers Association that we organise the 1st Congress of Writing for Galician Pipes, so that all together we drafted a document that was unanimously approved.

I remember that in order to explain the writing system I chose a Galician jig with Ricardo Portela's ornamentation, as the old master was there. I was very young then and I was honoured when he called me a few days later to ask me to write his version of 'Aires de Pontevedra', as he wanted to show off before his classical musician friends the complexity of Galician pipe music.

What attracts me to the Great Highland Bagpipe is primarily the sound. I think that the 'Scottish Stradivarius' who reinvented the sound of the pipes in the 19th century were geniuses. They renounced things like the second octave, semitones obtained through special fingerings, and looked for a powerful sound instead, escaping from the nasal and sometimes unpleasant sound of older pipes, evolving towards an elegant tone with the 'problematic' frequencies cut. Sound engineers nowadays might say it comes equalized. I think it's also very wise that gracenotes, instead of being defined notes with a strong presence as in other European pipes, just cut the sound, helping to articulate the music. Sometimes I feel as if it had been designed to listen to the music from far away.

Then there is the pipe band tradition, in which individualistic elements like vibrato, rubato, improvisation, notes with an uncertain tuning, are omitted in benefit of the ensemble. I think the Highland pipes nowadays, even if they are the same instrument in which pìobaireachd is performed, are mainly thought to work within a pipe band. The repertoire is unique too, especially pìobaireachd, even if there are links to other instruments or traditions, as my friend Barnaby Brown often discusses.

Even if military music is far from the spirit of fiesta of the Gaita, old pipers like Ricardo Portela realised that there were different levels of tunes. There was dance music and serious music just to be listened to. When I learn about old Scottish music, I find more and more things in common with old Galician music. Both seem to have been less rigid than we were taught. I can't forget probably the clearest similarity for an audience. Scottish jigs and Galician muiñeiras and the dancing with the arms up to the sky!

I love the Scottish tunes, from the mysterious pìobaireachd, to the 'Mason´s Apron' or 'The Clumsy Lover' that I played for years with the Chieftains. Another one I love is 'Aires Escoceses' composed in the XIX century by Spanish violin virtuoso Pablo de Sarasate, dedicated to his friend Scott Skinner. Known as the "Spanish Paganini", he put all his virtuoso technique to the service of the beautiful Scottish melodies as variations. I think he did it in a very natural way, unlike Beethoven, who I'd say suffered arranging Scottish songs as tonal tunes when they were obviously modal!

I would also underline its teaching system, especially the fact that the ornamentation is transmitted as a fundamental part of the body of the music and not as external ornamentation that can be improvised. This also exists in classical music in protestant countries. It would be interesting to find out the influence of Reformation in pipe music, maybe bigger than we can imagine. And then there is the influence of the British Empire and the Army. The glamour and the attitude of the Scottish piper might be a stereotype, but it still sells worldwide hundreds of years after being created.

In many ways Scottish and Galician bagpipes are strikingly similar. Hugh Cheape talks about an 'Atlantic corridor' that could have brought the pipes from Northern Spain to Scotland. Scholars say there have been pipes in Galicia for one thousand years, so who knows. There were historically many Scottish and Irish regiments in Spain, so there could have been some influence that way too. The fact is that looking at old paintings of Scottish pipes, or listening and playing to reproductions of the "Dale chanter" from the late 1700s, studied by Barnaby Brown, you could say it was basically the same instrument as old Galician pipes. I'd love to fulfil a long-time dream; a Scottish project integrating the whole Atlantic culture, as Scotland has managed to do for centuries.

I have had some amazing collaborations with Scottish pipers and pipe bands throughout my career. I remember wonderful concerts at Glasgow Royal Concert Hall with Flora MacNeill, Phil Cunningham, Donald Shaw, Alasdair Fraser, Fred Morrison, and the National Youth Pipe Band of Scotland.

We enjoyed the excitement and professionalism of the NYPBS so much that we played with them on many occasions. Fergus Muirhead brought them to the Festival in Ortigueira and to Vigo, where they played on the Carlos Nuñez y Amigos CD and

DVD. Then Fergus came and played with us at the Galician Festival at the Forum in Barcelona, and at the National Theatre in Dublin. And the National Youth Pipe Band came to play with us in Mexico.

Last year at Celtic Connections I played with the Scottish National Orchestra and a selection of young pipers, such as Finlay MacDonald. In Belfast I had as special guests the Field Marshal Montgomery Pipe Band the same year they were World Champions, and then in Dublin exactly the same case with the St. Laurence O'Toole Pipe Band.

When we play in football stadiums like the Stade de France, pipe bands are so important. And don't forget the soloists; I remember special moments there with great pipers like Robert Mathieson.

In my Breton album we make a dream true. We put together the Galician pipes (myself) with Scottish pipes (Patrick Molard) and Irish pipes (Liam O'Flynn) on the track 'The Three Pipers'. I am regularly in touch with pipers and researchers like Allan MacDonald, Hamish Moore or Barnaby Brown, whom I mentioned earlier on, and they are great sources of wisdom and inspiration.

In every special concert I invite pipe bands and soloists from around the world; USA, Mexico, Brazil, Argentina, Japan, and Europe. Sometimes they are just starting and when you come back a couple of years later there are two or three times more pipers and drummers. This is what I call "sowing piping". It is always great fun to play with the Scottish pipes, no matter if it is in small theatres or a big football stadium with hundreds of pipers from different countries. It's always relatively easy. If there is a piper with a sense of space, with a scenic feel, who can move, who can march, that's a Scottish piper. It's always a pleasure to have one or many on stage with us.

Introduction by Fergus Muirhead

I have had a very privileged life playing the bagpipes. I've played at London Palladium with The Chieftains and at the Vatican on the same bill as Chaka Khan and BB King. I've played with Carlos Nuñez in Barcelona and Dublin, and at Hampden when Scotland played England in front of over 100,000 football fans. I've piped in Tokyo and Tallinn, Barcelona and Bergen, Shotts and Stirling. I've played at the Russian Embassy in East Berlin with a Red Army rock band doing Beatles covers, and for British Ambassadors in Rome and Santa Domingo.

It all started because I picked up a chanter that belonged to my Uncle Hughie, a piper in an RAF band. My parents had moved to the New Town of Cumbernauld from Maryhill in Glasgow and I was attending Cumbernauld High School. One of the history teachers at the school, Ken Roberts, played the pipes and he started teaching me via the Boys' Brigade and then Cumbernauld Caledonia Pipe Band. I went to Hugh Wilson from Camelon for lessons at the same time as one of my neighbours, Roddy MacLeod, and started to compete in junior competitions alongside the likes of Euan Anderson, Colin MacLellan and Donald MacBride.

I had my first trips overseas with Cumbernauld Caledonia Pipe Band, torturous two-day bus journeys to festivals in Belgium and Holland, and my first trip to Lorient in the early seventies. Then, while at Glasgow University, I went to a concert one night in the Queen Margaret Union and heard a guy called Adam McNaughton singing a song about the Scottish football team going to play in Chile after the coup, 'There's Blood Upon the Grass'. There was a bunch of musicians there that night playing some tunes - John Gahagan, Mick West, John Byers, Jim Barnes, Jimmy McGuire - and they told me that they played in His Nibs and the Victoria Bar, both pubs in Glasgow, on a Saturday night. That was my introduction to traditional music and I was hooked. The rest, as they say, is history.

I joined Molendinar soon afterwards and the round of festivals and gigs started, all the time just as a hobby. I had a long discussion with Dougie Pincock and a bottle of whisky one night about the merits of taking up an offer to play full-time, but decided that it would be better for me to continue to pursue music in my spare time.

I have done so ever since. These days I spend more time speaking at piping events than playing at them, but I still find time to play a few tunes here and there, particularly in Catalonia where I sometimes teach the City of Barcelona Pipe Band as well. I also manage to get together with John Gahagan and Frazer McLellan as The Caulbums for the occasional ceilidh.

Compèring lots of concerts, every Piping Live! event since its inception in 2003 included, made me realise that there are some amazing people involved in piping with some amazing stories to tell, and so the idea for this book was born.

It's been a fascinating project. There are so many stories to tell and so many views which, while different, only help to accentuate the worldwide appeal of the bagpipe in all its various shapes, sizes, sounds and uses.

I hope that each piper's voice comes across in his or her tale. Each was told in a single sitting that flowed seamlessly and which I then turned into the words on the page. At the end of every conversation I had another hundred questions to ask the piper involved, and each chapter could be a book in itself.

I also hope that the book shows the huge versatility of the pipers, and of the instrument itself. The players highlighted on these pages have played competitions and concerts, recitals and receptions, festivals and football stadia. The have played for Popes and Queens, rock stars and film stars, as well as family and friends.

Many are involved with the pipes full-time as a means of earning a living, some simply play as a hobby. They are all at the top of their game in whichever field of piping they play and they all give at least some of their time free and as a means of encouraging others to participate. They teach, perform and compete with a huge degree of enthusiasm and professionalism

The list of pipers involved is my own, and the description of them as 'some of the world's top pipers' is also my own. It is completely subjective. I spoke to pipers who had interesting tales to tell, but there are many others out there with equally interesting stories to whom I didn't get the chance to speak. Maybe that's for next time.

Chris Armstrong

Chris Armstrong likes to say things only once. "One of my biggest pet hates is to have to repeat myself or to have to do something again. I always try to make sure everything I do is right first time. It started at school. I have always been very maths oriented and I was working very hard, I had surpassed everybody else in the class. The teacher decided this couldn't happen. It was creating extra work for her because I was so far ahead of everyone else, she put me back and made me do all the work again. Even at that young age I decided that I had had enough because this one person had really pissed me off."

Not only did that one incident create much of the determined streak that everyone in the piping world recognises in Chris Armstrong, it also changed the focus on what was important in his life, although it isn't necessarily a route he would recommend for others in the same boat. "After that incident I still applied myself but maybe not as much as I could have done and so piping took over from school work. Now I tell the kids I'm teaching that they shouldn't do that because it doesn't pay the bills. You need to get out there and study and get a proper job."

Chris's piping does now pay the bills since he is one of a growing band of professional pipers making a living from their music. It's a long way away from his introduction to the bagpipe. There was no family connection with the pipes; the young Chris Armstrong was initially attracted to them after a visit to Bathgate Gala Day as a five-year-old. "My first recollection was being on the Main Street and seeing the pipe band. It must have been the sound and the spectacle but I was sold on it and I kept on at my parents, telling them that I wanted to take up the pipes. The pipe major of the Torphichen Band at the time was a guy called Mark Bennett whose dad had a window cleaning business in Boghall. My folks must have got talking to Jim, Mark's dad, and told them I wanted to play. He told them I was too young at the time, I was only five after all. I kept on at my folks, constantly telling them I wanted to play the pipes."

Eventually Chris's parents relented. "I went to my first practice when I was about six, was handed a chanter, and taught how to play the scale. 'No bother', I thought and went home. I didn't put the chanter down for a week, it was in my hands all of the time. 'This is great', I remember thinking, but when I went back to play the following week it was a nightmare. I played up the scale, taking every finger off the chanter as I was going, and thought I was doing really well. I was told that it was all wrong. I was raging and devastated that I had got it wrong. I remember thinking that I was never going to do anything wrong ever again. So I went away and focused and paid attention. That feeling and determination has always stuck with me. I've always thought since then that you need to focus and be determined. To be good at this, there is no room for mistakes."

Wanting there to be no mistakes doesn't necessarily mean that there will be no mistakes, as Chris found out in an early foray into the world of solo competition. "I remember one of my first competitions, and I remember it because I made an arse of it. I played the first part of a two part 6/8 march three times. It was 'The Muckin' of Geordie's Byre', and I thought it was perfect because that was how I learned it, then I found out that I had played the first part three times — I hadn't even realised it! I was devastated because it was a mistake and it wasn't good enough."

As well as playing in the pipe band at this point, Chris had started taking lessons to improve his solo playing. "There was a guy in Bathgate who had been a pipe major in the Cameronian Rifles, John Matheson. He was the local guy who would teach the solo players. He came from a big piping family up Lochinver way. He rarely competed himself because of his Army career but I got introduced to him when I was about eight and he started me down the whole solo route which highlighted the need to be even better. Once you start to play in competitions you see what's out there and you realise that you need to work harder to meet the standard. John was teaching a lot of people at the time. It was a great experience. He had a lot of knowledge and a lot of patience. He was a very good teacher, very patient but very strict and good at getting the message across. You weren't frightened of him but you listened to what he said because you respected him. You did what he told you because of fear. A healthy fear, right enough."

Chris now teaches the pipes full-time at The National Piping Centre and the lessons he learned from his teachers all those years ago stick with him as he tries to pass his knowledge on to others, although it's not always easy with some students. "It's difficult when people haven't done the work. If I was teaching one to one and not through the Piping Centre then I wouldn't put up with it. It's a waste of time, not to mention the fee for the lesson. You have to strive to be better than the way you were last time in every single aspect of what you do. Because of that, if someone comes in to a lesson and they haven't done what I asked them to do, then I find that hugely irritating. It's a waste of time, time I could be spending on someone who wants to learn. It's slightly different at the Piping Centre because you can't turn people away. I can't tell students that they can't come back so I have to deal with it. But the student knows that I'm not happy. I don't necessarily shout and I certainly don't swear but I'll let them know. The tone of my voice or my body language will tell them that I'm not happy."

Chris thinks that this approach has given him a bit of a reputation amongst his fellow teachers. "It's funny, you speak to the guys here and they'll tell everyone that I'm the crabbit bastard on the teaching staff. To a degree it's true because I don't take any nonsense. An example would be some of the kids you get on the summer school. Some of the teachers will say that they are having a nightmare with a particular student and I just can't see it because I've obviously made it clear that there will be no room for nonsense in my class. I think it's part of the whole teaching thing. You have to have that presence to get the attention of the people sitting round the table, there's no point in putting up with somebody arseing around when you have three or four other people in the room. I suppose I'm a bit of a nutter in that way but that's the way I like to conduct a lesson or a class. It's so that the student knows that I'm there to do a job and they are there to improve. I don't have a magic wand, I can't make them better. I can help them, and I can give them advice and point them in the right direction, but I can't make them better. They need to do that for themselves."

For a number of different reasons, not everyone can do it. "It happens all the time that you'll meet someone you can't help. The worst thing is when you get someone who is mad keen and works and practices and puts more effort and time into it. It's frustrating when there is nothing you can do for that individual. The analogy I use is that I am completely useless at football. It wouldn't matter how much I practiced or how much time I put into it. I won't get any better, and I just know that I won't. You can't tell someone who puts a lot of time and effort into something that they're useless. It's a tough one. I don't feel sorry for them but I feel a bit of sympathy because they clearly want to do it but maybe don't have the ability. They're never going to attain the level that they would like."

Chris would prefer to be able to continue to teach these students, but reckons that there comes a time in some situations when you have to call it a day, although he is keen to draw a distinction between the way it happens with individual lessons and in the band environment. "It's not in my nature to tell them to just chuck it because they're wasting their time but it gets to the stage with individuals that you have to. In the band situation I haven't really had to do it because they generally figure it out for themselves since I am so demanding as a pipe major. I'm not in the habit of telling people they are not good enough. I'll try to encourage and tell them they need to work harder, and that's because my folks were always encouraging me. I try to do the same for others."

You won't be surprised to read that ending up as a pipe major has long been part of Chris's master plan. "I've always had a clear set of goals and ambitions with regard to pipe bands, and I always figured that at some point I would become a pipe major. I never saw myself as just a player in a band. I was pipe sergeant at Torphichen before I gave up the band for a bit to concentrate on the solos. I really enjoyed the work of putting a medley together, setting the pipes up, and getting a sound from them. That helped me prepare to get to the pipe major stage. I had been pipe major of a novice band, Seafield and District, when I was about eighteen and they did reasonably well. That was a good experience, teaching kids and helping them get on, and that was useful when it came to teach full-time."

Chris's determination is most evident today in his work as pipe major of Scottish Power Pipe Band. He had been pipe major of David Urquhart Travel just before the call to Scottish Power came, and he feels it important to set the record straight about his departure. "At the time I had just resigned as pipe major of David Urquhart Travel and there were a lot of people out there who think I jumped ship, but I didn't. I had already handed in my resignation so the timing made it look bad but I'm not in the habit of deserting things, it's not in my nature. I had decided that I had gone as far as I could with the people I was working with, and with that set up, at that time."

The appointment process he had to go through to get the Scottish Power job was one of the most difficult interviews Chris has ever had. "Roddy MacLeod decided to resign and I think that they approached four or five people. I don't know who those people were and I wasn't that interested to find out, but Peter Hunt called me to see if I would like to put my name in the hat and go through an interview process to be considered for the post. There was an interview in a hotel conducted by eight people, including Roddy. I haven't had many interviews and this was one of the most gruelling hours I have ever spent. I left with a splitting headache. Question after question after question. 'What is your vision for the band, what do you see happening, how will you work this?' I'm not used to that. I'm getting better at it because the position demands it now but at that stage it was very gruelling. In another way it was also great, because it gave me a chance to talk about all the things I could do to improve the band. Even that was difficult because I had to do it with the person who was leaving the post sitting there."

Chris obviously impressed the interview panel because a day or two later he got a phone call to say that they would like to move onto the next stage. "I had to go through another interview with an introduction to the Sponsorship Manager at Scottish Power and the Chairman of the band who was one of the Scottish Power people. They wanted to meet and suss me out. That wasn't quite as bad but still nerve-wracking because that whole thing of dealing with people was new to me. I've never really been one for putting myself in situations like that. I'll get up on stage and play in front of people no bother but that's a completely different thing."

The Scottish Power people were obviously just as impressed with Chris as the interview panel because they recommended him for the job. That was when the hard work really started. "I wanted to put my own stamp on the band and it took quite a while to do that, not because of what had existed before but because I had to go through the process of getting the personnel. In the first season the band only had sixteen pipers and about half of them were existing players. I took maybe six or so with me from David Urquhart who were all good players and I knew what they were like. It was difficult to begin with because the guys who were there were used to the way things were and had a way of working. I completely changed things, me being me."

Chris didn't make changes for changes sake. "I changed because you have to believe that your way is better, otherwise what's the point? I have a certain way of doing things and that's not negotiable. I have tried it and tested it and it works. I believe in these systems that I put in place because they work. I think that side of me comes from my first job as an engineer, and I have quite an organised head and train of thought. Anything that I do is not done without it having been tested to destruction before I do it. I started using my own tried and tested methods because then you get everyone singing from the same sheet."

One example of the systems Chris introduced when he took over at Scottish Power was the way he set the band up. "I don't go to a band practice and hand out new chanter reeds. I will have played every single chanter reed and chanter that goes into the band for at least half an hour before the piper gets it. What that means is that we don't waste any time at a band practice, and I hate wasted time. I can't stand standing around for any length of time. I'll set up chanters during the day, either by coming to work early or doing it during my lunch hour, and I'll play them each for half an hour. That way I know it's a good reed that's going in and if the person I give it to comes back and says it's not working properly then I know he's done something to that reed. That did happen for the first wee while because maybe the guys thought that my head zipped up the back. People will chance their arms but that very quickly stopped because it's all about control, and systems, and if you don't work with the system you get caught out. When I handed the chanter over it was working and was bang on and the right strength for the piper I gave it to, so if he comes back the following week and it doesn't work then that could mean that he or she had not played it, or has squeezed it, or shaved it, or moved the band on it, or wet it, or something like that. If that person had done something with that reed then they don't practice with the band that night because they're wasting my time."

"It's all control and expectation. I'm there, and put time and effort into the band, because I love it. If someone else is not putting at least a tiny percentage of the effort that I put in then I don't have time for that. It's a waste of my time and I don't suffer it. The person just doesn't play with the band. Simple as that. It all helps towards the smooth running of the band. I don't care who the person is. It was tough to begin with because I was a young guy. I was twenty-five or twenty-six at the time and dealing with older people was difficult. I've got a lot harder as I've got older."

Chris's band practices follow a routine as well, although strangely, for a man so wedded to routine, that may change depending on how well he feels the band is doing, or, more importantly, on what he feels needs to be done. "Typical band practice is two hours. During the winter we will practice for two hours because we're learning new tunes and trying to get the pipes going. During the season last year in the build-up to the major championships we would get the pipes out for forty-five minutes and go home again. The reason for that is this whole system and control thing. We're all doing the same things at the same time and the guys know the tunes. So you get the pipes out, get them up to pitch, tune the drones, get the drummers through, run through your competition sets and you go home. It should be forty-five minutes. If you have the right things in place it allows you to do that."

Chris reckons that the hard work should be done long before the competition season approaches. "If you think of how you would prepare for a solo competition, all of the hard work is done through the winter. If you have to stand for two hours a day practicing on the week of the competition then there is something far wrong. Get the pipes out, get them up to pitch, tune them, go through your tunes and put them away again. There is no reason why it should be different for a group of thirty people."

It only works, Chris believes, because he has the controls in place. "The way the system works with me handing out chanters is that short of a reed being a bad one, in which case the process starts again, all I require my guys to do is to play their pipes on a daily basis for fifteen minutes. That's all I ask them for because I make sure the chanters are going. That's my job, my responsibility. If I allowed people to go and muck about with reeds and set their own reeds then I don't have control over what's going on. It's not that I don't think they have the ability; it's not that at all. If they didn't have the ability they wouldn't be in the band. The whole point is in having control over what's happening. When you have twenty chanters to set you need to have control. If I move a bit of tape on a chanter and come back to it two weeks later I'll know what I've done, because I'll have taken note of it. If someone else has done it then I won't have a clue where it was. It makes my job easy, and it makes their job easier because all they have to do is play their pipes."

To dispel any notion that he is in fact running his band along the lines of a dictatorship, Chris does allow a bit of flexibility, but only so much. "I don't really have a problem if they just move a bit of tape but I hate it if the reed is taken out of a chanter. Once that happens, the connection between chanter and reed is lost to my mind and I don't trust it any more. I would change it. If the guy has been playing it every day and I have to do something drastic to it then there must be something wrong with it. It would do my head in. The week of the World Championships this year I think all I did was move half a dozen bits of tape. The day of the Worlds was different because it was really hot and that's a different set of circumstances. You have to adapt. I can tune twenty-seven guys in fifteen minutes on the day because it's all controlled."

Chris is happy to admit that not all of his ideas are original. "A lot of what I do is based on a study of Richard Parkes. I've been watching him now for a while from a distance, and learning. Just picking up wee things here and there. Field Marshal Montgomery is the band to beat and if what they are doing works then you try it and you adapt it and you make it your own. I know that is what he is doing and with the size of his band he has a couple of guys helping him on the day. I did have that but I changed it this year because the person who was helping me isn't with the band any more. I have looked at it again because I will have thirty-three pipers this season and it will be impossible to do it all myself."

So are the systems and controls and changes all having the desired effect? "We achieved the goals we set. My main goal was to improve on our placing in the Worlds from last year and we did that. Next year's goal will be to win a major so we'll see how that goes."

As any business guru tells you, and it seems to apply equally to the pipe band world, you need to set your goals with care. "The big goal for everyone is to win the Worlds, because that is the main title. But you have to be realistic with the goals you set. Way back at the start the goal was to win the Worlds but that's not going to happen in year one. Realistically I think we can now if we work hard enough but it all comes down to us doing what we need to do. There's no point in saying we got a second last year and a third the year before so we're going to win next year. We got a second last year and that's it. We need to work towards being even better and if we achieve that then we can win the Worlds."

Winning a major championship is not just about Scottish Power Pipe Band, it's about the other bands they have to compete against week in and week out. "At this point our major competitors are any other band that is capable of making the prize list. You can't narrow it down to two or three bands. There is this perception that there are the top three, but any band can be knocked out of that top three at any time. You can't just say that we are a top three band because we got three second places last year. That's not the way it works. It's like the solos. You go out and win a competition one week and play exactly the same the next week and you don't win."

As well as being recognised as a top pipe major, Chris Armstrong also has a prodigious reputation as a solo competitor, although he does blow hot and cold on this part of his piping life. "I go through stages. Between the ages of sixteen and eighteen when I discovered drink I took a back seat from solos and concentrated on the band. Then when I got to eighteen I met Fiona, now my wife, and she sorted me out. She wasn't prepared to put up with me going out every night of the week and getting absolutely hammered. At the same time I fell out with Mark Bennett. I disagreed with some of the things that were going on in the band. I left the band at eighteen to focus on my solo playing and I was absolutely disgusted to find out that my playing was abysmal because I hadn't bothered with it for two or three years. I was more interested in playing with the band, having some craic with the boys, and going to the pub."

True to form, Chris spent three months that winter dealing with the problem. "I registered with the Competing Pipers Association, got graded, and decided I was going to blitz the Highland games and get to Oban. I started taking lessons from

Andrew Wright for pìobaireachd. Before that I'd never really bothered my arse with it because I hated it. I realised that to be any sort of serious competitor you had to be an all-rounder so I started working on my technique. It wasn't about liking pìobaireachd; I just knew that I needed to play it. It was all about reaching the goal again. Through going to Andrew and starting to learn about it I did start to like and appreciate it. I was out of pipe bands from eighteen up to the age of twenty-four. During that period it took me three years to get a track record that was good enough to play in the Silver Medal. I worked really hard trying to get out round the games and win prizes, understand it, and get better. It started to pay off on the light music side of things. When I put my mind to it, I went round the games and started winning prizes. The year I was nineteen I got into the B Grade for light music and I qualified for the B light music at Oban and Inverness and won it. I got upgraded to the A Grade for 2000 and I won it, and then played in the Former Winners in Oban and won that. I think that's the first time that anyone has won the B, then the A, then the Former Winners in succession."

Chris was delighted that all of the hard work and focus he'd put into his music had clearly paid off and people had started to stand up and take notice. "Before that I was just a pisshead who was kidding on in the solos. Then in 2002 I had a bit of a breakthrough in the pìobaireachd and was runner-up in the Silver Medal at Oban, which was great. Then the following year when I was playing in my first Gold Medal I was lucky enough to win it."

For a man who puts so much faith into planning and preparation, and controls and systems, it may seem strange to hear him saying that he was 'lucky' enough to in one of the most sought-after prizes on the solo circuit. But as usual, where Chris Armstrong is concerned, there's a story behind that win. "I thought people were out to put me down but once I got out of the whole band thing I realised that wasn't the case and I was quite focused on the solo thing. I'd been banging away at it and had played at the Former Winners' March, Strathspey and Reel the night before. I got nothing and got pretty annoyed about it all so I went to the bar and got completely smashed. When I woke up the following morning I felt like death warmed up and had it in my mind that I wasn't going to bother playing. Fiona persuaded me that I should so I went to Eden Court with my pipes in the box, got them out and tuned them up. To be honest I don't really remember my performance because I was still steaming but I've heard the recording since. The pìobaireachd wasn't one of the most inspiring tunes on the planet but I made a good job of it and my pipes, for once, stayed in tune for the whole performance. I spoke to a couple of people when I came off and they reckoned I had played well and should be in the hunt. I didn't really think that much more about it because at that point I was still quite insecure with the whole pìobaireachd thing."

Thoughts of gold medals were far from his mind as he sauntered back to the Eden Court Theatre later that day to hear some of the other results. "I hung about to hear the result from the Hornpipe and Jig and on my way down to see the results I bumped into Jimmie McGregor. He said, 'Let me be the first person to shake your hand and congratulate you.' I asked him what he was talking about and he told me I had won the Gold Medal. I was genuinely shocked but I went for a look and there you go. So that's why I said I was lucky enough to get it."

Stuart Cassells

Stuart Cassells has always been a performer, and is quite happy to admit it. "I have always wanted to be the rock star of the bagpipes. I always wanted to perform and I really enjoy it. I had the experience from a young age of having an audience of a hundred or so to perform to every night; that's five hundred people a week from the age of twelve. I learned then what would work with an audience. You would try something one night and if it doesn't come off then you don't get the same applause. The sound of applause becomes quite addictive, you get used to hearing it and the more you hear it the more you like it. I have no problem admitting that I'm a bit egotistical and I think if you are going to be on stage and put yourself out in front of any audience then you have to have a level of confidence. An entertainer has to have some sort of ego."

The ego has to be tempered with some sort of talent, and there is no doubt that Stuart has plenty of that. He started to hone it from a young age, and was strutting his stuff for friends and family long before he first picked up a set of pipes. "I suppose I've always been a bit of an entertainer. From the age of five or six I could recite Burns poems, tell wee stories and sing songs. I would go to my Gran's most Sundays and she would ask me to sing a song or tell a joke. There were always people visiting my Gran's house so you never knew who was going to be there on a Sunday afternoon to perform to. I think I was better at poems than songs; unfortunately I've never really been much of a singer. Everyone knew me as a wee confident boy who could perform, so even through school I was the one who would be asked to perform in the class whether it was at Burns Day or the school show."

None of Stuart's close family played pipes, but his dad attended Queen Victoria School in Dunblane around the same time as the MacDonald brothers from Glenuig. The school insisted that pupils became pipers, drummers or Highland dancers, but the choice of which was theirs not yours. Stuart's dad was in the Highland dancing group, and Stuart is eternally grateful that he wasn't forced to follow in his Dad's graceful footsteps. Instead he took him to Wallacestone Pipe Band. "Tom Anderson was pipe major and his brother Peter was leading drummer. The band was in and out of Grade 1 at that time. It was very well respected and had great links with Brittany and in particular Bagad Kemper. It was a very musical band. I started when I was seven in 1987, having been rejected three years earlier because my fingers were too small for the chanter. I was taught by Willie Davidson, a former member of Muirhead and Sons Pipe Band. He was a disciplinarian and a bit unforgiving; he was a very strict teacher. Many people couldn't handle that authoritarian approach to teaching and it wouldn't be done much at all nowadays. If you hadn't progressed from the week before then he would tell you to go home and you wouldn't learn any tune or melody until you could play all of the exercises first to his satisfaction. I remember getting my first tune which was 'Kenmure's Up and Awa Willie'."

Stuart enjoyed his time in the pipe band world and played with a succession of others after leaving Wallacestone. "Wallacestone didn't have a Juvenile band, and I wasn't up to standard to play in their Grade 2 band, so I joined Craigmount High School Band and stayed there a year. Then the Royal Burgh of Stirling Band won the Worlds in Grade 3 and Pipe Major David Methven asked me to join them and to play in Grade 2. We had some good players, we thought we were going to win Grade 2 that year, but we didn't and the band lost a bit of heart and momentum so I joined Torphichen and Bathgate in Grade 1. I was twelve when I joined them and thirteen when I played in my first competition in Grade 1."

Stuart wasn't finished on his trip round the pipe band world, and he was looking for something special. "I've always been more into the music rather than the sport of pipe bands. The two most musical bands when I was growing up were the Vale of Atholl and the 78th Fraser Highlanders from Canada. I moved to Vale of Atholl when I was fifteen. At that time they were like my boyhood football club of the pipe band world. When I was learning, my dad bought me a tape from MacLeod Highland Supplies and it was the first one I had that wasn't military pipe band stuff. It was called No Reservations and it just blew me away. The Vale became the band I would follow when I turned up at competitions and they were the band I wanted to play with. I also became a big fan of Gordon Duncan. Young Andrew Wright, whom I competed against in solos, was in the Vale of Atholl already. I got on really well with him so I started attending Vale band practises and then I joined them the week they did the Pre Worlds concert at the Motherwell Civic Centre Concert which was recorded for the CD Live and Well. So my picture is on the CD sleeve even though I didn't play at the concert - although Andrew Wright played my pipes in his brilliant solo."

While Stuart was having a great time playing in pipe bands he was also making a name for himself in the solo piping circuit.

"After winning the local chanter competition when I was eight I got the bug for competing. I was in a generation of some incredible young players. Chris Armstrong and Ross McCrindle at ten years old were unbelievable. There is a video of Chris on YouTube that my father took of him playing a strathspey and reel at the solos in Bathgate when he was ten and even still, listening back, it's pretty much faultless. It wasn't until I received serious solo tuition from George Lumsden when I was that age that I started to compete at the same level. It took me two years to eventually beat Chris in a solo competition. Thankfully after that I started to win quite a few. I think I won most big junior competitions and also a few seniors. My highlights would be winning three Mod gold medals and the day I won every event at the SPA amateur competition. In my first year in the seniors I got placed at both Oban and Inverness in light music and in the Silver Medal at Oban. I'll always feel very thankful to have received pìobaireachd tuition from Donald MacPherson for a couple of years. I remember thinking what a fantastic player he was even at that age. I played on the CD released in 1997 entitled Young Pipers of Scotland which also featured Chris Armstrong, Andrew Wright and Gordon McLean."

Perhaps as a precursor to what was to come in later years, Stuart managed to get lots of practice by entertaining tourists in the Stirling area. "My uncle was the chef in a restaurant that had American tourists in on a Friday night. Their regular piper was a young guy called David Methven, an excellent player who was with Shotts and Dykehead at the time and who went on to become pipe major of the Stirling Band, which is how I ended up there. He couldn't make it one night and so my uncle piped up and said that his nephew played. He gave me a call and I had forty-five minutes to get ready. I became the regular fill in for David and within six months he was too busy with other things and they gave me the job. I was working with an old guy called Chick Duthie, a real character. He was a great after dinner speaker and he did the best 'Tam O'Shanter' I've ever heard, and I've heard a lot. I learned from Chick about how to talk to an audience and he became like a surrogate father. He was the head guide at Stirling Castle and he gave me my first job when I left school. That was another great experience and a great way of learning how to communicate with people. I suppose that's where I gained the confidence to be able to go on stage, become a showman and talk to people from all over the world."

As well as developing performing and communication skills by playing regularly for the tourist market, Stuart was also coming to realise that playing the pipes might be more than a hobby for him, and that meant he would have to think about more than just the music. "I was getting very busy performing at functions so I set up a company and had to pay tax. It's a good thing to pay tax, you know. There are a lot of musicians that are scared of it but I think it's a good thing. It gives you a responsibility to society and it gives you a responsibility in your own profession."

Thinking about tax and setting up the company also allowed Stuart to consider other aspects of what was rapidly becoming his full-time job. "You have to think of all of the aspects of being a musician. It's not just about playing, you have to think about where you're performing, how you're going to get there and how you're going to look when you get there. It gives you a little bit of credibility if you are a musician who can properly market yourself, and if you're going to properly market yourself then you have to pay tax."

It's a lesson that he believes a lot of other musicians should learn. "If a musician wants to be successful then they have to know the product. We certainly got that right at the Red Hot Chilli Pipers because we knew what we were selling, who we were selling it to, and we treated it as a business from day one."

The ability to recognise that what you're doing has become a full-time occupation rather than a pastime is something that also needs a bit of work according to Stuart. "Scottish folk music is confused over the difference between hobby and work. You have musicians who essentially play folk music and that, by its very meaning, is informal. We now have musicians on stage at the Glasgow Royal Concert Hall and if you're going to go on stage there then you can't dress the same as you did when you were playing a session in a bar. You can't speak the same way, or play the same way. A lot of musicians haven't learned to make that jump from being hobby musicians who play a little bit at night in a ceilidh band to becoming professionals. The ones who have become successful professional musicians on the Scottish folk music scene have not necessarily been the best musicians. They have been the best professionals, and there is a difference."

At the heart of that difference is the ability to put on a performance. "You can't go on stage and say 'I've just met Jim in the bar so I thought we'd get him up for a tune'. If someone has spent thirty pounds to come and see you in the Concert Hall they want to see a performance that you have actually thought about and have rehearsed for and dressed for and that you're presenting properly and professionally, in exactly the same way as they would associate other genres of music being performed and presented."

Performance has been central to the band that Stuart

founded and has travelled all over the world with — the Red Hot Chilli Pipers. Performance as musicians rather than as pipers and, as far as Stuart is concerned, there is a world of difference between the two. "The idea came because I used to play at a lot of corporate engagements and there was a band doing the rounds called The Gutty Slippers. I would be playing as a traditional piper dressed in full number ones and maybe doing the 'Address To The Haggis' and this band would come on and dance around for twenty minutes and make more money than I did — and I was there all night. They looked to be having a lot of fun as well. They weren't the greatest pipers or drummers but they captured the imagination of their audience and were very busy. I thought, wouldn't it be great if there was a group of pipers and drummers that could go to corporate events like that, where we're imposing our music on people who haven't bought tickets to come and see us, but we can let them hear what the bagpipes can really do."

Stuart was frustrated because although the bagpipes could do some pretty amazing stuff, the public very rarely got to hear it. "I was a member of the Vale of Atholl Pipe Band when they were known as being the most innovative pipe band in the world. We were the best concert band to go and see in those days. It was phenomenal and yet whenever we played in front of regular punters we would play 'Scotland the Brave' and 'Killiekrankie'. I used to wonder why we weren't playing 'Steam Train to Mallaig', 'Il Paco Grande' and all of the other concert pieces we used to do because people would have loved it. The only reason they cry for 'Scotland the Brave' all of the time is because that is all they know but if we gave them the opportunity to hear other stuff they would love it."

Stuart had an idea that you could treat the bagpipes like a rock guitar and get rid of the formality. "There's nothing wrong with formality, but there is another side to the bagpipes. The bagpipes weren't invented for the military and they weren't invented to play in front of a judge all the time. Not that I have a problem with either of these two uses since I've done both in pipe band and solo competition."

The band name came about by accident. "I was studying at RSAMD, living in a student hovel in the West End of Glasgow, and my flat was in a bit of a mess. My girlfriend at the time and I were doing some tidying up. My CDs were all over the floor and she was helping me put them in genre order. About two in the morning I was looking through all of my piping CDs and in amongst them I found a Red Hot Chilli Peppers CD and asked her why. She thought it was Red Hot Chilli Pipers. So at two o'clock in the morning I had a 'Eureka' moment and phoned up my friend Willie Armstrong and although he thought I was bonkers at first, when he heard the name he was in. I had loads of contacts with the entertainment agents I had worked with as a traditional piper and so pretty much the next day I started getting us gigs. Along with Willie Armstrong there was Brian McLaughlin, who both played in Royal Burgh of Stirling Pipe Band with me at the time. The original drummers were Gavin Ogilvie and Steven Graham. Gavin was leading drummer of Stirling Pipe Band when I was pipe major and Steven was in the same year as me at the RSAMD. We were the five original members. Brian decided to pack it in after the first three gigs because he didn't think there was going to be any money in it. He sold his kilt and decided he didn't want to do it anymore because we had done the first three gigs for nothing. Gavin took an opportunity to travel the world in a campervan. Then Kevin MacDonald joined us and Malcolm McEwan took over the percussion role. I wonder if Brian ever feels like the fifth Beatle?"

The first few gigs that the Chilli Pipers played were done for nothing, confirming Stuart's view that you have to give something away to start to make a name for yourself, but you also have to know that you have something that people will want to pay for. "The turning point, when I started to think it would work and we might make some money from it, was a wedding we played. I think it might have been Malcolm's first gig. It was in Edinburgh and we had to do a kind of traditional bit during the day and then go back at night after the meal. We went down to the Grassmarket for a few pints and that day Wales were playing Scotland in the Six Nations Rugby. The game was in Wales but there were lots of Welsh fans in Edinburgh and so we ended up playing in a bar. The punters were going crazy. We spent the afternoon trying out new material and things we had never even practiced before. Malcolm brought a different groove to the band with the quad drums and djembe. The stuff we were playing was going down really well so after a few beers and a few tunes we went back to the wedding. We were on top form and blew the wedding apart. That's when I thought, 'We've really got something here'. We'll jump on chairs and get right into people's faces. It's bagpipes but not as people know it. It's not formal and it's a new style. And it's played well."

The Chilli Pipers are not without their critics, and there are many who say that what they have done to bagpipe music is sacrilege. Stuart Cassells holds no truck with that view. "We were able to use pop and rock songs that people could identify with as a hook to give them a reason to listen to the pipes. We were looking for a new audience, a wider audience than the one that was listening to Scottish music. These people wouldn't normally listen to bagpipes, so we had to give them a reason. We were doing something interesting by playing other types of music on the bagpipes. When we want to listen to opera, when we buy Russell Watson, Michael Bublé or Katherine Jenkins, every CD has 'Ave Maria' and all of the classics that people can relate to and then once they're hooked they can start to appreciate some of the finer opera pieces."

"This is what has happened with the Red Hot Chilli Pipers. By blending pop and rock songs with good traditional bagpiping and tunes by Gordon Duncan and Fred Morrison I hope that we have brought people to the music who otherwise wouldn't have been into it and we've allowed them into the piping world. Hopefully these people will discover great piping events taking place across Scotland like Piping Live! and they'll become fans of other groups, whether it's the Battlefield Band or the Treacherous Orchestra."

As far as Stuart is concerned nothing should be out of bounds for the Chilli Pipers, or for anyone else who want to push boundaries. "Music is music at the end of the day and there's no such thing as right and wrong. There is good and bad music but that's not the same. It can be to your taste or not to your taste. I don't mind if people don't like our music personally, or my style of playing. I suppose I was a generation after Fred Morrison, Gordon Duncan and Allan MacDonald who very much changed the way pipes were played by adopting a style similar to uillean pipes, and they weren't respected at all for that by their peers. They were, all of them, lambasted by the traditional piping world, and I've heard from many trad pipers that Gordon Duncan and Fred Morrison couldn't play a march, strathspey and reel. To me that's rubbish. I've heard both of them play incredible march, strathspeys and reels. Fred is proven on the competition circuit and has no need to explain himself to anybody. I was in a generation just under them with guys like Finlay MacDonald and Chris Armstrong. We looked at what these guys were doing and idolised it. It was more acceptable by the time we started doing it. I think me, Finlay, Lorne MacDougall, Ally Hutton and Ross Ainslie have all proved the case that you don't need to have a track record in competition now to be respected as a good piper and musician."

As well as the pipers mentioned above there are another few that Stuart believes deserve mention because of the material they have introduced. "It's very clear to me what a legend is. A legend is not only a great player; a legend is someone who has changed the music and repertoire for their instrument. In that category there are only a few pipers like Donald MacLeod, GS McLennan and Gordon

Duncan. Tunes like 'The Little Cascade' and 'Mrs MacPherson of Inveran' by GS McLennan changed the way we played, and the way we embellished tunes. Donald MacLeod, with tunes like 'Susan MacLeod', was different again. He composed tunes that were unique and which have stood the test of time. I think there have been great composers who have composed great tunes but who didn't change the style of tunes we play on the instrument or change the way the instrument was played. Perhaps Peter MacLeod would be an example? He wrote great tunes but he didn't change how new tunes were written."

Although Stuart has thrown away the music book, and the rule book, as far as the Chilli Pipers are concerned, he has a slightly more conservative view of the way that pipe band competitions should be run. "I think the Chilli Pipers and other groups should be free to go wherever they can and it's up to the audience to decide whether they like it. When it comes to pipe bands, however, I'm quite conservative. I don't want to see pipe band competitions with guitars and drum kits and lots of backing musicians playing along with the band. To me that defeats the purpose of it being a pipe band. To me a pipe band should be only bagpipes and drums."

Having set the scene by determining the make-up of a pipe band, Stuart does then back-track a bit in terms of repertoire. "What you do with the bagpipes and drums is a different question. I would like to see the medley competition starting without two three pace rolls. If it starts with a solo piper followed by the rest of the band then that works for me. If the band wants to start with the drummers playing a jig groove then that's fine. If the drum corps wants to use snare drums with rope tension or have two or three bass drummers that's okay as well. If you have your pipers cutting out half way through the medley and let the drummers take it away then do it. If a pipe band wants to play in a concert during the week of the Worlds they should be able to do so and add whatever instruments they want and that they thinks add to their music. Then they should go back to the definition of the pipe band — and that's pipes, snare drums, tenor and bass — for the competition at the weekend."

Stuart's life as a touring musician is over, due in large part to an on-going medical problem with his hands called focal dystonia but he has great memories that will remain with him for the rest of his life. "We did some amazing gigs with The Chilli Pipers. We've played all over the Far East for Chivas Regal whisky, staying in the best five star hotels and at the best parties. We've played for many celebrities including The Queen, Sir Paul McCartney and Ewan McGregor and we've performed at the biggest festivals in the world, sharing the bill with musicians from Bryan Adams to Iron Maiden. My personal highlights were performing to thirty thousand people at The Gathering in Edinburgh in 2009 and winning the BBC One prime time Saturday night talent show called 'When Will I Be Famous'. I also loved the tours of the USA we did."

He's keen to point out, however, that the romantic notion he had of a musician's life touring on the road had to be revised, at least in the early days. "Whenever the band start a tour we all have these great fitness plans and imagine that we're going to come back like Greek Gods, then three days into the tour reality strikes. You have to eat what you're given on tour, or you don't eat at all. There's also drink available all the time so you have to restrain yourself from just drinking every night. When I was at RSAMD everyone on the course had this romantic idea of what it was like to be a touring musician and thankfully I've had the opportunity to experience it, and to experience it at quite a good level. It's not as though we were living out the back of a transit van. We have nice tour buses and we stay in nice hotels, but even at that the romantic idea was blown out of the window pretty quickly."

"It was real Groundhog Day. We get up and have the same thing for breakfast every morning. On the last German tour we travelled five hours, arrived at the hotel, checked-in, did a sound check, maybe managed something to eat, then an hour or so to have a wander around whichever German town we were in and then turn up, get ready, play the gig, finish the gig and dismantle, and if there are people hanging around after the gig we might have a wee party, then it's bed and the same thing the next day. I enjoyed it but touring's not quite as glamorous as it's made out to be."

Stuart thought at first that he might continue in some sort of non-playing role with the Chilli Pipers. He eventually stopped playing but was frank enough to admit that he would miss the kick that goes with being on-stage. "I did think that there could be a management role in the Chilli Pipers, but applause is an addictive thing. When I started the band I was the only ego but by the time I stopped playing everyone in the band had an ego."

"We had an amazing journey but towards the end there was a clash of characters and a debate about where the band was going. It becomes very frustrating when you've created something that is then going in a different direction from the one you would like it to take. It also gets very hard if you're not performing on stage and you're not the superstar piper any more. It was easy when I was the superstar piper in the band because what I said went. The rest of them weren't as well-known as me or could play the way I could. The minute I started to get problems playing due to the focal dystonia, a couple of people used it as an opportunity to take over the glory of the frontman role. I'm being quite candid here but that's essentially what was happening and that was making it extra difficult to come to terms with my condition."

So Stuart is looking forward to a life post-Chilli, but a life that will almost certainly involve music. "At the moment I'm still finding my feet. I'd like to be involved in music. It's where my friends are and I've had a lot of fun and good times with music. I love it, I love piping and I would like to continue to contribute in some way. It's an unfortunate development that my dystonia means I can't perform any more but it would be a real shame if I couldn't continue to contribute something."

"When things settle down with my real job and I get used to getting up in the morning and going to it then I think I'd still like to do some teaching and I'd also like to be involved in the media side of things. I think that I helped the Chilli Pipers find a media platform for piping and I'm comfortable doing that, and I'd like to continue to do that. When your mortgage doesn't rely on it then it gets a bit easier to give your time for free and you can enjoy it more because you're not dependent on it."

Red Hot Chilli Pipers

Willie Armstrong has been with the Red Hot Chilli Pipers since the beginning. "Kevin MacDonald and I played in the Stirling Pipe Band with Stuart Cassells and we had an idea that we would put a band together to do corporate gigs. We had all being doing weddings at Cameron House but it got to the stage where we were doing it every weekend, standing around waiting on photographs to be taken. It was quite boring. We had an idea that if we played a twenty minute show with our mates it would be a hell of a lot better. No-one knew us at the time, so all of these early gigs that we did were done for nothing. No fee."

Stuart Cassells has already recounted the story of the name, but he missed out a bit in his version. "Stuart called me at three o' clock one morning and said 'Willie, I've got a name for the band.' He was that kind of guy, when he got an idea he had to share it with you there and then."

Willie was only half-joking when he said that the reason for the band coming together in the way it did was boredom with the traditional wedding, and the waiting around that it usually entails for the piper on duty. "When Kevin, Stuart and I did weddings with Scottish Bagpiper we used to muck around with tunes because we were bored, and so were the punters listening to us. Every now and again the photographer would tell me to stop playing for a minute and it was because nobody was listening. It wasn't until we started playing 'Eye of the Tiger' and stuff that we had a laugh with the crowd. That's the hook. You can play traditional music all day long and not get the same response. There is a value in us playing the rock covers because it gets people who are not interested in bagpipes to become interested."

The band's real big break came when they won the BBC talent show, When Will I Be Famous. Kevin MacDonald reckons that they never in a million years thought they were in with a chance. "Stuart saw an advert in one of the Sunday papers for the show and he went to audition with Malcolm and Gregor. They were delighted when they discovered that they had got on to the pilot. We went to London in January 2007, just for a bit of craic. It was not like today's talent shows. There were eight rounds. We were up against a choir of young boys in the first and we got absolutely destroyed. They had one hundred and one home viewers and they selected their favourite, after which it went to the public vote and the top two acts got into the final. We thought we had no chance. We were playing the bagpipes for goodness sake."

It wasn't a wasted trip however, since Kevin and the rest of the Chilli Pipers managed to combine the talent show with a pretty special gig. "The following night we played at Ewan McGregor's Burns Supper in St Martin's Lane. We did the TV show one day and then the next we got to meet Sir Paul McCartney, Lulu, Sharleen Spiteri, Ewan McGregor, Ronan Keating and Yasmin Le Bon."

They were so sure that they had no chance of qualifying for the final of the competition that Willie Armstrong felt confident in making an offer to the rest of the band. "We were up against a band called String Fever in the final and one of the guys in that band was going out with someone that was in Blue Peter so we knew we had no chance. So much so that I told the guys that if we got through I was going to donate my left testicle to the band. Well, not only did we get though, but we eventually won the competition, so my left testicle belongs to the Chilli Pipers."

Although the band went down to London to have a good time and not to think too much about winning, Kevin remembers that Stuart Cassells was slightly more stressed than the rest of the band. "The good thing about getting on the show was that there was no pressure on us. Apart from Stuart that is. We told him that we were there to enjoy ourselves and it didn't matter if we got bits of our choreography wrong and he was going crazy telling us we needed to get it all right."

The band was especially keen on getting their choice of music right. Willie was unhappy when the production team tried to have a say in the choice of music the boys played. "The production team wanted us to play 'We Will Rock You', and other rock covers. They could see the value of that, and so could we because, to be fair, if we didn't do it we wouldn't have been on national TV at eight o'clock on a Saturday night. The producers listened to our set which was 'We Will Rock You', 'The Eye of the Tiger' and 'The Clumsy Lover'. It was really important to us that we got 'The Clumsy Lover' in, but just before we went on they asked us if we would play the 'Eye of the Tiger' for longer and drop the pipe tune. To a man we said that we weren't prepared to do that and if we had to do that we wouldn't bother. We stuck to our guns and I think that helped. That was the bit the judges loved; you could see that from their reaction."

The Chilli Pipers noticed that something was different

almost as soon as they returned from London. "In September 2005 we got booked to play twenty-four party nights in the Albany Hotel in Glasgow. We got seventy-five pounds per person per night to do a half-hour set and we thought it would be great if we could sell a few CDs as well. It cost us three thousand pounds to record so we put in five hundred pounds each. We got one thousand cut and were all so proud of it because it was our first CD. It was the most embarrassing thing in the world trying to sell them after the gig; we tried it and hated it. We had a company distributing our CD and they were taking orders for ten and twenty at a time. Then the day after the TV show I got a call with an order for five thousand to go straight to HMV and places like that. We had to get them made in a week, it was crazy."

The craziness hasn't stopped since the win. It's been a roller-coaster ride that has taken them all over the world several times and to gigs that many people would have thought impossible for a band made up of bagpipes. Kevin MacDonald is an accountant by profession so he gets to look after the band's finances, and reckons that he effectively has two jobs now. "I have my own accountancy practice as well as playing in the band but I do them both full-time. There are no days off! Because I'm self-employed I can juggle my time but we turn over just under one million pounds a year and we've sold quarter of a million albums so that has to be seen as a very serious business. There is bottom line profit but we re-invest that in the musicians and in the stage show. We've just bought new stage gear to take to the USA this year. We've signed major deals to take the band coast to coast in the USA and also a deal in China."

All of this touring, on top of a very busy corporate schedule at home, has meant a bit of restructuring for the band. "We had to move it away from just Kevin and Willie and Stuart and present it as a brand so that if one of us wasn't around the audience wouldn't know the difference." As Stuart has mentioned, he has had his own problems and is unable to play now, so that meant even more of a restructure.

Even though this means using more and more musicians as time has gone on, Willie believes that the quality of the music can't be allowed to suffer. "It's the Red Hot Chilli Pipers. The bagpipes will always be in tune and any musician who comes to join us needs to be as good, or better, than those already in the band so that the quality will keep going up and up. We don't use a big drone sound, for example. We only ever have one drone miked out of three sets of pipes and that gets put into the sound mix, but the rest are perfectly tuned. We still tune our drones and take as much time doing that as we do with our chanters."

Stevie Lawrence, a very well respected musician on the Scottish traditional scene, has been involved with the Red Hot Chilli Pipers since the early days, and he agrees with Willie Armstrong about the quality of the music. "They're not the first band to use rock instruments and bagpipes but where their slant is slightly different is that it is more like a pipe band with a rock backing, whereas a lot of the other 'bagrock' bands, if you want to use that term, are rock bands with pipes, and there is a difference in the way that the music is arranged. The fact that they have three pipers opens up the possibilities for seconds and harmonies whereas a lot of the other bands only have one or two pipers and they are playing the same thing. Their piping is not so heavily arranged as the Chilli Pipers. The focus with the Chilli Pipers is the pipes, and that's what brings the punters in."

It's not only the desire to be playing perfectly in tune that means that they have to be perfectly in tune, according to Willie. "We know that there are people waiting to knock us down, and they have done in the past. They call us a joke act or a cabaret act that has gone wrong. We might be that in some traditionalist's eyes but we can all play the pipes. Musical preference is so individual. Pipe Band players are very supportive, and a lot of them understand what we do, and that we play the pipes correctly. If we let that slip than that would be a problem. Even at midnight, when we know there are no pipers in the audience, we still spend the time to make sure they are right. One night at Gleneagles we thought there would be no pipers in the audience and then we discovered Iain MacFadyen was there, so you have to be on your toes."

Willie also believes that the Red Hot Chilli Pipers have done a great job in advancing the popularity of the bagpipes in Scotland in recent years. "I would challenge any musician in Scotland to have done more to get kids interested in traditional music. We haven't done it single-handedly if you think about the government programme of getting traditional music taught in schools. They want to play 'We Will Rock You' on the pipes and I think it's right that we have kids involved. I think that out of learning 'We Will Rock You' they will also learn the pìobaireachd and the marches and my argument is that you wouldn't get the chance to play that without 'We Will Rock You'. If he's playing 'We Will Rock You' then at least he's putting a set of bagpipes under his arm and playing."

Stevie Lawrence agrees. "Once you make rules about music you are limiting not just your audience but the music itself. An instrument is an instrument and as long as you do what you do well it's good. There is a kind of snobbery, not just with bagpipes. The uillean pipes went through the same thing and it wasn't until people like Davy Spillane and Moving Hearts came along that it really moved the music on. It's the same here."

"There is a kind of closed attitude that says you can only use instruments in a certain way, you can only listen to bagpipes when there is some guy walking over a misty moor playing them. If it works it works, and that's what the Chillies have proved. You can't deny the publicity the Chillies have brought the bagpipes. We see it at the merchandising stall at gigs, and, no offence to any other pipers out there, but a lot of the kids want to learn the pipes because they have seen the Chillies. If we are encouraging other people to learn then we are doing something right. I was a rock player and what turned me on to trad music was bands like Steeleye Span and Lindisfarne. Today, kids are coming to see the Chilli Pipers and a lot of people who come to see us are into rock music and they've never seen the bagpipes being used like this, and that's great."

Ian Duncan

Many of the pipers in these pages have talked about the fact that they never once paid for a lesson when they were learning and they now feel uncomfortable that they have to charge their own students. Ian Duncan goes one step further. "I would cycle five miles to Fyvie to get the bus to Banff and then I would have a two hour lesson from Jimmy Robertson. Jimmy had been a pipe major in the Gordon Highlanders and was the main teacher in the whole of that area. He wrote loads and loads of great, mainly unpublished, tunes. His most famous one is 'Farewell to the Creeks' (the Creeks are at Portknockie in Banffshire), and Hamish Henderson wrote the words to 'The Banks o' Sicily' to the tune. Jimmy would give me a sixpence at the end of the lesson. I didn't pay him, he paid me, and I would go into town and spend it. Nobody paid for lessons in those days and now that I'm retired and give private lessons I find it really hard to take money from people because I have never paid for a lesson in my life. But that's just the way it is now."

In another twist that most teachers would find a bridge too far these days, Ian was made to write each tune down as he was learning it. "Every time you got a new tune you had to write it out and bring it back to him the next week. My first tune from him was 'Kate Dalrymple' and that's quite a hard tune. I think he saw it as more of an exercise, and I had to write it with a quill pen on a big artist's manuscript book. I had to draw the lines and the stave and it had to be a pen dipped in ink, pre fountain pen. I had to write every tune, so I've never had a problem writing music."

The phenomenon that was the Vale of Atholl Pipe Band takes up a large part of Ian's story, but he had to go through a few moves of house and teacher before joining the band. "When I was thirteen the family farm wasn't doing well. When my Dad was in the RAF he was taught electronics and when he came back after the war he started wiring barns because electricity was coming to Aberdeen. He joined the Hydro Electric Board and we had to move to Caithness. We stayed there for two years and I did second and third years at Thurso High School. I didn't really have a piping teacher there so I was just ticking over, although I kept playing with Turrif Pipe Band in competitions and would come down to play with them and get lessons from Bill Hepburn, the pipe major. That was it until we moved to Pitlochry. Dad got into the power stations when we moved there and he took me to Bob Brown for a lesson."

Bob Brown decided that Ian wasn't ready for him yet and sent him to Dr Kenneth MacKay at Laggan. "Bob told me to come back and see him once I had six tunes. I went up to Laggan from Pitlochry. Kenneth was a great teacher who had really resurrected piping in the Laggan area because there was nothing happening. He was a retired GP and taught a hell of a number of kids in that area, so much so that when he did pass away there were all these kids and no teacher, and the local authority ended up getting John McDougall into the schools to teach. I went to him for two years and then I went back to Bob and continued to do so while at Aberdeen University studying electrical engineering."

Ian is quick to admit that Aberdeen wasn't chosen as a place to study purely on academic merit. "I went to Aberdeen largely because Jack Taylor and Bill Wotherspoon were there already and I had been seeing them at the games. Both have Gold Medals now and I think Bill is Chairman of the Piobaireachd Society. They are both doctors as well. We went to Bob Brown for lessons on the bus into Braemar until Jack got his car. Bob passed away soon after that and so we went to Bob Nicol instead. By this time we were into Gold Medal tunes, there was no Silver Medal then. There weren't that many pipers in those days so there was no need for a Silver Medal. I enjoyed lessons from the two Bobs, although they were completely different. We got an awful lot more work done with Bob Nicol. Bob Brown was a family man, you got your lesson and that was it. With Bob Nicol, he was on his own and you could be there all day covering lots of material, even although you only went to play one tune."

After university Ian ended up at Teacher Training College in Dundee. "I had done my degree and I didn't really know what I wanted to do so I applied for teacher training. I was too late to apply for Aberdeen and had to go to Dundee. I was just about finished my teacher training when the headmaster of Pitlochry High School phoned me and asked if I fancied a job. That wouldn't happen nowadays, it would have to be advertised. He said that his wife was a maths teacher at the school and her mother was really ill so she needed to be at home looking after her, and I got her job at Pitlochry High School."

Within months of coming back to Pitlochry, Allan Cameron, the pipe major of Vale of Atholl Pipe Band, decided to retire and Ian was asked to take over. He had played with the band before he went to University. It was the local band in those days and didn't compete. "It was a town band that played for tourists and we got paid for it. We got ten bob for every engagement because we were playing for these masses of tourists and that was the only entertainment for them."

The first and most important thing Ian did was appoint someone to help him teach the young players coming through the band. "The best thing I ever did was ask Allan Cameron to teach. He was technically such a great player and he taught loads of other great players. They include Gary West and Malcolm Robertson. Malcolm played with the Vale for years, then Saint Laurence O'Toole, and is now in San Francisco. Ian also taught Sharon Walker, and Stevie Saint from Wolfstone. I get the credit for it sometimes and continually have to correct people. It was really important that Allan was there doing the teaching because it allowed me to focus on the band. I just couldn't have spent all these hours teaching these kids with everything else I had to do, and if Allan hadn't been there to do it I'm sure the Vale wouldn't have grown into the band it did. I took over a band that only had two people younger than me and the standard was very poor. I did find it hard and we lost quite a few bodies early on because I think they realised it was going to be hard work. I was going to make them try to play a bit better."

In order to help them play better, at least in the short term, Ian had to employ a few 'special' teaching techniques. "I had to teach them to cheat a bit with certain things they had to miss out. If in doubt, leave it out, as long as you cut the note hard enough or hold the note long enough. It works in the band, but it wouldn't work in the solo world. It certainly worked in Grade 4 which is where we started when I took over in 1974."

When Ian took over the band they didn't compete, but that soon changed. Success came very quickly. "The band's first competition was in 1976. We won Grade 4 at the Worlds in 1978 and we won Grade 3 in 1979, in Nottingham, which was a two day event incidentally. Then we hit Grade 2 and we were first in piping and last in drumming."

As often happens with bands, the quick progress through the Grades was impacting one half of the band more than the other. Thankfully for Ian, help was at hand. "We struggled on with our drum corps for a wee while, maybe two years, just trying our best. Then I was contacted by the leading drummer in the Pride of Murray Band in London, John Moneagle. I was beginning to lose heart by then and I think that if John hadn't joined us I would have decided that I had taken things as far as I could and gone back to the solo world. But John coming in was great. Every second weekend he and his father-in-law and two other drummers drove up from London for a practice. In 1983, even although we didn't win Grade 2, we got promoted to Grade 1. The standard was so high that year that they promoted three bands; us, Toyota and 2nd Battalion Scots Guards. Toyota won, Scots Guards were second and we were third but there was such a gap between the three of us and the rest of the bands that we all got promoted. The Vale was the only band to survive in Grade 1 though."

The band was delighted to be playing in the top flight, but in some ways Ian's heart wasn't in the world of competition. "We got a sixth place in Gourock in 1986, then, after numerous runner-up prizes, gained our first championship in Grade 1. By 1988 we were developing a concert repertoire. Our debut was in Ballymena and I think that the concert was becoming more important than the competition. I honestly believe we could have won the Worlds if we had played the game a wee bit safer. It wasn't us. We loved the music and folk came to expect us to change our medley every year and to play new and exciting tunes. I believe competition does stifle music. For example, look at the fuss made of the three pace rolls at the start and 'Oh dear, that band had a bad start' and the big 'E' at the beginning. That should be a minor detail."

Vale of Atholl were always likely to move into the concert arena from competition, but some of the judges' comments maybe helped that move. "We were one of the first bands to use different pitched tenor drums and John K McAllister said, 'Good intro but where are the Indians'. 'I'm not deducting any points for this dreadful drum corps, but the point of it is to accompany the melody, not create a different one', was another comment."

But the most amazing adjudicator's sheet Ian has from his time at Vale of Atholl is the one where the band got seventy-six points out of seventy-five. "In those days you had to put down your points and then give your sheet away. One year a judge had given the first band sixty-five out of seventy-five but then the bands kept getting better and better and by the time we came on he had already given seventy-five so he gave us seventy-six...and then got banned."

The competition set-up hasn't changed for years now and Ian believes that it's maybe time to do something different. "They have tried the semi-circle and a few other things. I would have the Grade 1 bands static on steps or a stage, pretty much as they do it in Lorient, in front of the main stand in the football stadium, and let them give a ten or fifteen minute performance. We are the only musicians who don't face our audience, we're awful anti-social. It's not right, and we need to move on. I think Rab Mathieson had been an advocate of that for years."

Although Ian was pipe major of The Vale of Atholl Band, he has acknowledged that he couldn't have done what he did without the help of others. He's already mentioned Alan Cameron, but it would be impossible to tell Ian's tale without mention of his brother Gordon, sadly no longer with us. "Gordon spent a lot of time putting together the tunes for the medleys. He was also great at helping the other pipers in the band. He would quietly take guys away and adjust reeds or whatever needed doing, but he did it quietly, behind the scenes and without a fuss. I once dropped Gus Clark and Gordon took him away, gave him a reed, and sorted the problem. Before I knew it Gus was back playing with the band. Gordon just had such a great way with people and I was kind of more ruthless. I would just have told him 'your reed's out of tune you're not playing.' That was the way it worked."

In a classic case of good brother, bad brother, Ian was happy to play the baddie. "If you're about to go on and there is something wrong with a reed you're better just dropping the player. You can't really take a reed out or move a reed without it being unsettled for ten minutes or so, and it's maybe a confidence thing as well. You've lost confidence in that piper or that reed and he maybe needs a new reed, or a wee chat. I don't remember any resentment, although there may have been some in the background that I didn't know about. I once gave one piper a hell of a bollocking because I had dropped him and he said, 'Yes, I can go to the beer tent now'. 'No, that's not the attitude; you should be desperate to play', I replied. I have to confess that I might not have used those exact words."

While Ian was giving some of his players a hard time, Gordon was encouraging the others, especially the younger players in the bands, such as Ross Ainslie, now a prodigious player and composer in his own right. Ross says, "I could hardly play, maybe just a few tunes on the chanter, but Gordon would take me aside and got someone else to run the band. He just really took to me. I don't know whether he just saw something in me but after six months I got a prize for most improved player. I was practising all the time. It got to the point that it was football or music and music won. I had football trials for Scottish Schools, but I was just more into my music pals rather than my football pals. We won the Worlds with Vale of Atholl with Gordon, and then I went into the Grade 1 band when I was eighteen."

Ross wasn't only impressed with Gordon's ability to help him out in the band. "I suppose if you go to any session these days you are pretty much guaranteed to hear at least five of Gordon's tunes over the course of the night and it's a shame that he's not around to hear that. He was a great composer and of course he had that maverick spirit. He took his bagpipe and created the Gordon Duncan style of playing; it's amazing the way he managed to do that. For the likes of me and Ally Hutton, as younger players, it was really exciting. I remember when he brought the Circular Breath album to the band and we just thought it was amazing. It was so new and we were excited to get it home to listen properly. There were other people doing things but Gordon's stuff was just so exciting. I love 'The Belly Dancer' because Gordon had a Jock McCann chanter and he could get this B flat note only on this chanter. It's like a B with the pinkie down and he sculpted a tune round this note, it's unbelievable. One of his best compositions."

Ian and Ross still work together today with the Gordon Duncan Trust, as Ian explains. "Gordon left tons of music because he started tunes and then didn't finish them. There is no name to lots of them, but I'll get a second opinion from Ross, he knows his work well. We're determined to get another book out and I think there are about twenty tunes we know of so far. There were lots of other tunes that he made his own, Irish tunes in particular. Some of them didn't really fit the pipes, but he made them fit by bending notes and half covering holes. The trust is ninety per-cent book sales, we've sold four and a half thousand so far, a great achievement for a piping book. We're also selling a couple of CDs that Ian Green from Greentrax put together. We've had a few concerts in Perth but they don't make money, the last one lost £1,500 because the hall is so expensive to hire. The Trust exists to help young musicians and so is a great legacy for Gordon."

Ian has great memories of his time with The Vale of Atholl, both on the competition field and in concert. "We had some great trips with the band. Santa Rosa Games was quite special because we beat Simon Fraser University that day and it was our first year in Grade 1. We didn't know who Simon Fraser were. I saw SFU and thought, 'Scottish Farmers Union, what are they doing here?' Triumph Street were there as well. We won on the Saturday and they won on the Sunday, and so they won overall when points were added together. It was our first year in Grade 1 and the audience went wild because they had never heard a Scottish band before. Although these memories are great I always preferred the concert stage to the competition stage, although I did still get a buzz playing at the Worlds and places like that because the punters wanted to hear the new tunes that the band were coming out with. Concerts were the thing and we did loads of them. We did the Beach Ballroom in Aberdeen and it was like being rock stars. There were all these girls from Deeside Ladies dancing about in the aisles, and we were signing autographs and the like. It was crazy!"

On occasions it felt to Ian is if the competition and the concert had merged. "We did three Ballymena concerts and they are fanatics over there, it was like being at a pop concert at times and they wouldn't leave you alone, but when they were sitting listening it was like playing to twelve hundred judges because they were very intense and very critical."

Ian spent twenty-seven years in charge at Vale of Atholl, and in the end he just got tired. "I got stale. We had three bands, including the Juvenile and Novice Juvenile, and there were over a hundred people. I was just doing too much, so in 2000 I called it a day. I had been teaching pipes in Dundee since 1979. It did eat into my life and I don't know how I managed when I took over the band. I had no phone in the house. It took me about a year to get a phone in and then when I got it, it never stopped ringing."

The intervening years have brought changes. "I have old recordings of Muirhead & Sons and there is not a lot of difference in the togetherness of the band's playing between 1975 and today. It may be slightly tighter, but what is different is the sound. Technology and better reeds and drone tuners have allowed the sound to improve dramatically. We never used drone tuners in the Vale, well I never used them at all, just tuned them all one-to-one to me. The low As might all be slightly different. Ideally they would all be the same, but often the low As are not absolutely bang on, but the drones will all be the same. Drone tuners are used by everyone nowadays and maybe that is a confidence thing, but it also allows one person to tune the whole band. It's not without problems however. The piper feels you on the tuner and adjusts their blowing. So when you go to tune a set of drones they might blow a wee bit harder. You have to go back and do it again gently and without them knowing you are there!"

While technology has improved the sound that bands can achieve these days, Ian is concerned with the pitch that bands are playing at. "I'm hoping the pitch won't go any higher. In fact I'd like it to come down. If you are lower pitched than the other bands round about you then you can sound a bit dull in comparison. When you have a higher pitch it is brighter and I think that's why it happened. We have gone back to concert pitch with the Atholl Highlanders. We were out in Bermuda and I got a set of chanters from Chris Armstrong. It was just wonderful. We were playing with a Military Band so we had to be playing in B flat and it was great. We got so much more colour and harmonics from the drones, they just weren't as thin as they would have been at a higher pitch. Especially in B flat, it's just much more vibrant, and where the pipes are meant to be. It's the pitch I played at when I was younger. I don't know how far back we would have to go to get the pipes back down to the key of A. Quite a long time I would think."

Even although Ian doesn't much like the pitch that pipe bands play at today, he is impressed by the sound of the instrument generally. "Very rarely do you hear a bad instrument these days. I do a lot of solo judging and the quality of the instrument is so much better. In the seventies it was really unusual for someone to get through a whole pìobaireachd and have their drones in tune at the end of it, it was the exception. Not today. A lot of the solo players are still using cane so I think it's the accoutrements and drying agents and whatever they are all using that makes the difference. All I can ever remember is a wee thing in the blowpipe, just a wee cord with a tube that caught the slavers. I still play a sheepskin bag with a cane bass and Eezydrone tenors. I got the first Gore-Tex bag that was ever made. It was pink and huge and I had to try to hide it because it was sticking out the back of my cover. That's the only material it was available in, the pink."

Although Ian personally prefers sheepskin he is impressed that others manage to get a sound out of a Gore-Tex bag. "The drones sound more alive with sheepskin. Then you get people like Angus MacColl who confuse me because he plays Gore-Tex and gets as much life out of his drones as anyone using sheepskin. Maybe it's just the combination of a stunning set of pipes and great reeds. Alistair Gillies always played Gore-Tex. I'm a really dry blower and I think you need some moisture in Gore-Tex, and that's maybe why they didn't suit me. I've become a dryer blower as I get older, I don't know if that's a general rule or not, but I'm definitely much dryer now than I was. Maybe it's all the bad living; whisky and stuff."

Finlay Johnston

Finlay Johnston likes his practice to be as close to the real thing as possible, and he's even found a way to get nervous when he's practising at home. "I try to imagine myself on the stage and if you can do that then I think it's a real benefit. If you can get yourself in that frame of mind when you are practicing then you can actually feel a bit of nerves creeping into your playing and I think that's a really good thing. You've got to have a pretty good imagination but I think that little bit of nerves gives you an edge and perhaps that little bit extra that you might otherwise struggle to get. I try not to think about anyone else and what they're doing. I'm trying to concentrate on all of the things that Ronnie McShannon, my teacher, told me when we've been in a lesson and I'm trying to get into the groove. I think that if you let other things bother you it's no good. I don't try to think about what others are thinking about me, for example. I try to concentrate on the music and anything else is secondary."

Although he has good ideas for his practice sessions, Finlay reckons that perhaps he should have more of them. Practice sessions that is, not good ideas. "I'm pretty complacent when it comes to practicing and I often leave things until the last minute. It's quite frustrating and I often wish I had given myself more of a chance, but at the same time I think that I work better when there is a bit of pressure. In terms of the Gold Medal or The Glenfiddich preparation, where there are set tunes to learn, you need to make sure that you give yourself enough time to get your head round them, learn them properly, and get into the tune. In terms of the length of time taken to learn a tune it varies but I think that most people would aim to have their tunes off in January with a view to playing them in August or September in competition, but considering there is a lot to do in between it's tough."

Like many top competitors, Finlay understands the difference between 'learning' a tune and 'understanding' the tune. "You can actually learn a tune in a very short space of time but to actually get into it and understand it takes time. Ronnie McShannon and I will get the book out and he'll talk me through it and tell me how he thinks it should be played, and how he would interpret it. I'll sit down and go through it, play it myself and he might pick out a few bits and pieces where he thought I wasn't doing it right. Then I'll go away and try to learn it, come back a couple of weeks later with it learned, and then it's a case of going through it with a fine toothcomb, picking out phrasing. That part is on-going. Learning the tune is easy, learning to play it well and interpreting it is where the hard work starts. Ronnie has a real natural touch with pìobaireachd and he will tell me the different ways it can be played. Nine out of ten times I agree with the way he's going and I know that he has had first rate tuition, so for me to argue with him would be pretty ignorant. We agree on most things really and have a good relationship."

Finlay points to his first appearance at The Glenfiddich Championship in 2012 as an example of the support that Ronnie McShannon has provided. "I struggle to reproduce what I do at home on the stage and I sometimes let nerves take over but Ronnie has been absolutely brilliant at helping me get over these things. Ronnie is also the main man I go to for pìobaireachd and light music. He was delighted that I got a prize first time out. We had both decided that my goal was to go and do my best and not let myself down, to get a fourth place in the light music was great."

Although Finlay has always relied on Ronnie for the bulk of his tuition, he is fortunate that his mother, Anne, plays as well. "My mum is pretty switched on. She was a good player and is musical so she does have a very good ear. She was also a successful competitor. John Wilson, when he introduced me at The Glenfiddich, said that on the day she held her own against a lot of the guys. At home when I'm playing she's always listening and giving her opinion. When I finish practicing I know that there will be a voice that will shout out and she'll give me some of her, not always well-received, criticisms. I do know she's right, one hundred percent of the time she's right, and I'll take it on board, but that doesn't stop me moaning about it first. I'll go back and tell her and I think she does appreciate that. Dad has quite a musical mind on him as well and he's great for tune choice. He always remembers the tunes he played in the bands and the support I've had from them, and from Ronnie, has been great."

It wasn't only Finlay's parents that were involved in the piping world. His grandfather was a piper and started him off on the chanter on long summer holidays on Tiree. "Initially there was a chanter sitting at the side of the fireplace in our house so it was natural for me as a kid to pick it up and fiddle about with it. My grandpa used to come and stay with us periodically throughout the year, he was from Tiree. He was also a piper and he taught my mum, and I think that with his influence it was inevitable that I would play. My dad was a drummer so was a bit outnumbered. I think that I picked up a chanter before I could even get my hands round it. It was natural that I wanted to try to play, and as soon as I was big enough they got me my own chanter. I think I was about seven and a half or eight years old. When I used to go and spend the summer with my grandfather, my mum would come over for a week and then just leave me, so I would stay on Tiree for five weeks and that's how I started properly."

His grandfather may have started things off but Finlay was soon making up his own mind about his tuition. "I'm too young to remember this, but my Dad and Ronnie have always been close, so what happened was that I just said one day, when I was about eight, that I wanted Ronnie to teach me. I've no idea why I said that, but that's how it all started, and he's been teaching me ever since. Pretty much since my first tune he took me on and he has given me so much over the years. He has been there every step of the way to help me."

The support Finlay has enjoyed has helped him to produce a very successful run of competition success in the solo events, and he's pretty clear on what he has enjoyed most so far. "Highlight would be either the Gold Medal or the fourth place at The Glenfiddich. In fact even just playing at The Glenfiddich was great. I came off the stage on a real high. Just being on the stage, walking out there and seeing the audience, knowing that you are playing to a really switched on audience, probably the biggest I have played in front of in a competition, was just great. The whole thing was a great experience; I can't put it down to one thing. Even if I hadn't won a prize I would still have loved it."

As well as a hugely successful solo piping career to date, Finlay also enjoys the time he spends with Inveraray and District Pipe Band, although he does accept that there are pressures in trying to combine both worlds. "There is something to be said for playing in a band but there is no question that it is time consuming and it can distract you from your own thing. I find that I've really got to keep on top of my own playing when I'm with the band because it is very easy to switch off your own style and your own thoughts and do what the pipe major is asking you to do. When you have new tunes to learn and it coincides with learning a pìobaireachd then it can be quite difficult to balance it out. I don't always deal with it very well at the best of times. I just try my best to fit it all in."

As well as finding the time to fit it all in, Finlay has to keep telling himself that there is a difference between playing in a band and going solo. "Solo style is completely different from playing march, strathspey and reel in a band so you have to be observant and not fall into the little habits that you might get away with in a band. It's easier to hide in a band. The band style is definitely more up tempo from the way I would play it on my own, and maybe a bit more clipped in places, whereas in the solo stuff you maybe try to keep it as open as possible. I think that most people would agree that it's a completely different style playing in a band as it looks for different qualities."

He counts himself lucky that this difference is not as big an issue with Inveraray and District as it might be with other bands. "One thing with my band experience is that one of their main strengths is the focus on musicality and that does benefit me. In the band it's not just a matter of playing at a hundred miles an hour and getting through the tunes, they are always thinking of how to make it musical as well. So it's been good and bad for me."

The good obviously outweighs the bad, and Finlay has now been with Inveraray and District Pipe Band for close on six years. "I had expressed an interest to play with them before then but I couldn't because they were in Novice Juvenile and I was too old. They have had a remarkable rise through the grades and I think it's purely down to good leadership and a great work ethic. They all look up to their leaders and they really trust them. If they are asked to do something they just go and do it, there's no kind of ego. If Stuart Liddell or Stephen McWhirter says do something then they do it. It's not been easy. Stuart and Stephen have worked with these kids since they were pretty much starting out to get them to Grade 1 standard. I don't know how Stuart does it. He can adapt on any level to pretty much anything; he's really good that way. I think that they can go the whole way and win the World Championships. When, I don't know, but it won't be in the distant future. "

Finlay works with his father Tom and Ronnie McShannon at Pipe Dreams, and this, together with his family's piping background, means it's no surprise that he's really into the pipes he plays and how they are set up. "I have two sets of pipes but I have one set that I've been playing a lot recently. My mum played a set of old silver and ivory Hendersons. They were bought from Peter McFarquhar and they are the sister set to the ones that were Pipe Major Angus MacDonald's pipes. I also got another set, MacDougall's, which were my grandfather's pipes and they came from somewhere in Tiree. I'm not sure of the exact history, but my uncle had them. I asked him if I could have them for playing in the band and he gave me them. They are a great set of pipes but I just find it a bit tough to keep two sets going and that's why I don't play them very much. I have played them in the solos once or twice but right now I'm just using the Hendersons."

Finlay finds that with a bit of effort he can make one set of pipes fit his band playing as well as his solo work. "I use a different chanter for the band but the drones are set up quite well and my chanter reed for the band is slightly harder than the one I use for solo work, but not by much, so I can get away with playing the same set of reeds. My own chanter is quite low in pitch at the moment and my band chanter is at the other end of the spectrum. I prefer a low pitched chanter for my solo playing. I think you get a wee bit more depth out of your drones if the pitch is a bit lower. Not too low because you don't want it to sound dull at all. I didn't actually set out to have a lower pitch. I just found a reed that I liked, that worked really well and that happened to have a lower pitch."

Finlay puts a lot of time into selecting the right balance of reeds for his pipes, but he's keen to point out that he doesn't spend his whole day looking after them. "It's not hard to get a set of reeds given what I do during the day but I don't spend all day playing pipes, I just work like anybody else. It certainly helps to work at a place that makes reeds. At the moment I'm playing a sheepskin bag with Ezeedrone bass and tenor drone reeds and an EzeePC chanter reed which my dad made. I've been playing it for two years and it's going really well, which is good because finding a new reed can be a nightmare. I find it really hard to pick out the qualities I'm looking for in the early stages. I'm looking for something that's well balanced, has a nice sound and hopefully, once it has a bit of moisture about it, can develop into a good reed, but it is tough to know sometimes and there is a lot of trial and error involved. I use my dad's reeds, and apart from a time at the early stages of my piping career when he wasn't making them, I've used them ever since."

Faye Henderson

It was never in doubt that Faye Henderson would play the pipes, although perhaps it started earlier than she would have expected, even for a family as steeped in the bagpipes as the Hendersons. "Because I grew up in a piping family and there was always piping going on around me, it would have been pretty impossible not to at least try it out. I was at an age when I wanted to do whatever my sister Fiona was doing and she was having chanter lessons, so I just sort of joined in. I kept going because I enjoyed it. Fiona eventually moved on to the fiddle and I stuck with the pipes."

Although it seemed a natural choice of instrument for Faye, she is keen to point out that she never felt any pressure from either of her parents to pick up a chanter. "They never actually asked me if I wanted lessons. I was quite young at the time, around four I think, so they didn't really get a chance to ask. I just did it anyway. It was a kind of fun thing to do after school. I came home and played the chanter. With Mum and Dad both working from home it was all too easy for them to give me lessons. They never had to make me practice, I wanted to do it. Because I was four my fingers were very small and Mum and Dad had to get a chanter specially made for me since there were some movements that I couldn't do on a full-size one. I couldn't do a birl for ages because my fingers wouldn't go over the chanter properly. I think I just enjoyed the challenge of wanting to get it right even from a young age."

Getting it right is important to Faye in everything she does, and the challenge that she speaks of is more important to her than winning. "Whenever I go to a competition it is never about winning, it is always about doing my best and realising that anything that happens after that is a bonus. That takes the pressure right off. You're not thinking about anything other than trying to be better today than you were yesterday and that is a fairly achievable goal if you just get in the correct teaching and practice. I'm not saying there's no stress. You want to make sure that your pipes are in tune and that everything goes smoothly but that's not pressure. From when I was young and we went along as a family to a competition, it was always good fun. If the hard work is done there is no reason to go and feel nerves or pressure. If you can do it at home then most likely you will be able to do it on the stage."

Faye has always, and only, ever had lessons from her parents, Murray and Patricia. "I have always been taught by Mum and Dad, I never felt the need to go anywhere else and it has all worked out nicely. When I have a lesson they are my teachers and all of the rest of the time they are Mum and Dad. It's easy to switch that on and off and they are not too different as teachers than as parents. It's still about giving advice and taking things on board."

They have obviously done a pretty good job teaching Faye. Two years ago she became one of the youngest winners of the Gold Medal at Oban. "I was eighteen when I won my Gold Medal. John Burgess and John Wilson were both very young, sixteen and eighteen I think. You appreciate it at the time but looking back you realise it was quite special. It opens so many doors to do other competitions like the Clasp and The Glenfiddich. Everyone aspires to play in these competitions so the Gold Medal is the first step in going into these other events. I was very happy with my performance the day I won my Gold Medal and that was good enough for me. Winning was just the cherry on top and I didn't expect it at all. I was expected to play in the Silver Medal at Oban and Inverness and I only got to play in the Gold Medal because James Beaumont withdrew and I was first reserve. So it was just a happy coincidence."

Winning the Gold Medal, while admirable in itself, is like starting over in some ways. "I'd like to get my march, strathspey and reel playing up to the same standard as my pìobaireachd and there will be a lot of focus on that from me now. When I was growing up my concentration was on pìobaireachd. Mum and Dad wanted to make sure the foundations were solid and they've done a great job. With all of the tunes I have had to learn for pìobaireachd I think my light music might have taken a back seat. Now that I have the time and I don't have to think about going round the games to get a pìobaireachd track record I can think a bit more about my light music. Maybe I can learn a few more tunes — I've been playing the same ones now for years — so I'll focus a bit more on this, while keeping the pìobaireachd at the same standard."

Maintaining the standard of her pìobaireachd at the same time as improving her light music is, for Faye, all down to practice. "Lots of practice is the best advice I can give. It's really important to feel comfortable with the material you're playing. Take lots of advice, trust your tutor, then take on-board everything they tell you. You need to have an opinion as well so if you're not happy with what you're playing you need to have a conversation with your tutor about how you can enjoy it more. If you enjoy it more then you're going to play better."

Faye Henderson

Faye has a well-developed and well-rehearsed practice routine. "You're always learning as you go but I think that you need to properly learn a tune before you start to play it perfectly on the pipes. Every time you play is a learning experience but thinking a lot about what you're going to do with the tune is maybe one of the hardest barriers because you need to know what you want to do with it before you start playing. You need to get to know the tunes and learn them so that when you actually get on the pipes it's a lot easier. When I start to learn a tune I look to see if there are any recordings of Mum or Dad playing it and if there is scope to change anything that I don't like in their versions. Is there a different way to interpret it? You're always going to have the things that you must do."

"You need to have your phrasing, and your technique needs to be perfect. I'll usually do what the book says but if there are certain areas that don't flow naturally then I'll look at other manuscripts. I normally use the Bob Brown and Bob Nicol style because that is what my parents were taught. There was a year in the Clasp where it was the Donald MacDonald settings where it was very different, and I really liked that. There were different movements and different ways to play some of the movements like the taurluath and crunluath. It was a different style of playing because the tunes were generally shorter and you could come back and play the whole ground again, not just the first line. It was nice to dip into that but it was also nice to come back to something more familiar."

Before the tunes can be learned and practiced they have to be chosen, and Faye has developed a fairly rigorous selection process. "For the set lists I'll look through all of the tunes and I'll mark the ones that interest me. You either have six or eight tunes and you have to pick three or four. So I'll go through the list and look at the manuscripts and mark the ones that attract me. Then I'll sit down with Mum and Dad and we'll discuss the ones I want to do. We'll look at the different settings and get their views on which ones I can bring most music out of. They are both very good at spotting the tunes that would best fit me. That's important because you have to pick the tunes that you think you make the most music out of, and the ones that you enjoy playing the most. Sometimes they are not the same! I can choose the tunes without their help but it's great because they have such a vast knowledge of how they are played. Dad has been playing so long that he has played most tunes and he knows what they are about. He knows what I would be able to do with them. We usually agree most of the time. When I was younger they would pick my tunes and just tell me

55

which ones I was learning. That was fine but as you get older and hear new tunes you start to think more about the ones you would really like to learn."

Practice on its own is not enough though. "Play at as many competitions as you can handle because that's where you learn most. That's where you learn to tune your pipes and where you learn that maybe your technique will suffer if you're under pressure so you adapt and think about your movements. The only way to learn about what's going to happen in a competition is to play in a competition. You've got to do what feels right. Some players won't like to play in as many competitions and if that's the case then that means plenty of practice at home. So find out what suits you and go with that."

While Faye obviously loves playing her pipes, it is not the be all and end all of her life, and she enjoys her down time as well. "Because of the way the piping competition season works you get a chance to take a break over Christmas time and January when there is not too much going on. There's never been a time when I've been constantly playing. I believe in working really hard during the competition season and then taking a few weeks off. That way when you get back into it you feel really refreshed and you don't feel as if you're slogging away too much. I think it's important to have a few weeks where you don't play at all because then you miss it and you come back to it forgetting how much you enjoyed practicing. I think that if you play constantly you can get stuck in a bit of a rut and not see the bigger picture."

Having just recently completed a Law Degree at Aberdeen University, the pipes were a great distraction for Faye. "During exam time it's great to be able to have a break from studying and go away and have a tune. It's relaxing, and you're not in the library looking at exam notes. Throughout the majority of university terms I'm not doing too much actual playing. It's more learning tunes and listening to things and then having a good go on the pipes, but not as much as when term ends and it's getting to summer."

A distraction is all they are ever going to be though. "I like piping as my hobby and I think that if I was doing it all the time I don't think I would enjoy it as much. I like having my own time and I love getting away and then coming back to it. It's definitely just a hobby and I get more enjoyment out of it that way. There's not the pressure of it being my livelihood and thinking I have to do well to be successful as a person. I like to have it separate. It would be different if I was a piper full-time and I needed reputation to get pupils. I'm playing for myself, that's all, and I find that quite relaxing."

As well as making a decision that she is never going to be a full-time piper, Faye has also pretty much decided that she is never going to be a full-time lawyer. "I'm not going to practice law or be a full-time piper and that's as far as I've got. I'm applying for a few positions in the business sector. I really enjoyed doing the law degree but being a lawyer was never really the end game for me. When I was in high school I wanted to do a degree that would challenge me. A lot of students who study law end up diversifying so I thought that doing the course would be a challenge and would give me a wide range of transferrable skills."

While Faye decides what she wants to do with her life the one thing she knows is that she will continue to play the pipes. Although improvement and being as good as she can be are up there as ultimate goals, the odd prize doesn't go amiss. "It would be fantastic to win the Inverness Gold Medal because then I wouldn't have two sets of tunes to learn each year. It's good to aspire to win things because you can set yourself a goal. Can I be good enough to win it? With Dad having six Clasps it would be a dream to have one of my own to add to that."

Unfortunately Faye won't have the opportunity to win that Clasp playing against her dad, but she enjoyed the events that they did play in together. "Playing against him was great. We competed in the Clasp for two years as well as in London and at Oban and that was a really good experience. When I was younger I always wanted to compete against him and he kept telling me that I could if I won a Gold Medal. He was still playing but I don't think he really thought I would win one before he retired. We always asked Mum for her opinion after we played but she stays pretty neutral. I think it was more stressful for her having to think about two of us. Now that Dad has retired from competition she only has me to think about."

Murray and Patricia should both be very proud of everything that both of their daughters have achieved, but as Murray himself says, it's down to the way they behave as a family. "We've always worked together as a team. That's why it's never made any difference who teaches Faye, whether it's Patricia or me, because we're both coming from the same place. Patricia has taught Faye just as much as I have and Faye is comfortable with that. I know it doesn't always work with parents and their children and I don't know why it's always worked so well with Faye, but it has. It's nice to see your children take that same philosophy as you, that if something is worth doing it's worth doing as well as you can. It doesn't really matter whether it's university, music or life. Faye pipes because she wants to, not because we think it's a good idea, and it's the same with Fiona and her violin. Fiona did start on the chanter and decided to learn the fiddle instead. That's great, it wasn't a problem at all and we've fully supported her through her fiddling. It's just nice to see children make the best of themselves, whatever that may be."

Murray Henderson

In contrast with the hundreds of pipers and drummers who fly all over the world these days at a moment's notice to teach, practise and compete, it took Murray Henderson five weeks to sail to Scotland in 1973. He was heading there to improve his piping, having taken it as far as he could in his native New Zealand. "Bob Brown came out and toured New Zealand and I was attracted to his style of interpretation. The idea was that I would come over here and have tuition from him, but unfortunately he passed away. The logical thing was to go to his good friend Bob Nicol."

Forty years later, Murray is still here, and loving every minute of his life. He recently retired from competitive piping and sees this as his opportunity to explore new challenges, as well as reflect on a career as one of the top solo players of his generation. Murray first retired nearly twenty years ago, but that only lasted for six years. "I was asked to share a recital at the National Piping Centre with Iain MacFadyen. I had such an enjoyable time preparing for that performance, and I was looking forward to playing on the same stage as Iain, whom I had competed against for about fifteen years until he retired. My preparation had to be thorough, and I enjoyed that aspect so much that I thought I might as well have another tune on the boards. I've competed again at places like Skye, Oban, Inverness, London, and Blair Castle. All indoors you'll notice. I haven't played outdoors since I came back from retirement."

Could this be another false dawn, as John Wilson suggested when introducing Murray's final march, strathspey and reel performance in the Great Hall of Blair Castle in October 2012? "No. This time, it's time. I've had a very enjoyable career. Well two careers really. Since coming back I've managed to win two more Clasps, so I think of it as two careers. You reach a point when the time taken to prepare has to increase in order to maintain your standards, and I always thought it would be nice to stop competing while still able to feature in prize lists at the major events. I had a pretty big birthday last year and that felt like the right time to stop piping competitively."

It all began for Murray when he was four years old. "My father played in the Timaru Highland Pipe Band and did a little bit of solo competing. My older sister was learning the chanter and I would watch her and see what she was learning. She would go off to school and I would take her practice chanter and tootle away, and then she would come home and wonder why her chanter was soaking wet. I just happened into it, I didn't 'decide' to learn the pipes. It was just something I did and it was all by ear at that stage."

Murray started playing in the mid-fifties and it was a good time for piping in his home country. "New Zealand has been very lucky with the number of top players that it has had, and a lot of that is due to the pipers who came over to Scotland. Lewis Turrell for example won the Gold Medal at Inverness in 1958. He was the first non-Scot to win one of the Highland Society of London's Gold Medals. He also won the Strathspey and Reel, and the Jig. Allan Dodd was also over from New Zealand and he won the March. So there you had a couple of young Kiwi lads in 1958 giving an outstanding account of themselves. Donald Bain was so committed to furthering his piping that he moved to Scotland for two years, 1967/68, with his wife and two pre-school children. Donald continued the New Zealand success by winning both the March and the Strathspey and Reel at Inverness during that extended stay, and went on the win the Gold Medal at Inverness on one of his subsequent trips in the seventies. That shows the strength of piping in New Zealand and as a youngster I was hearing that standard of piping on a regular basis."

It wasn't all one-way traffic. "You had Scottish pipers emigrating to New Zealand. Angus MacAuley emigrated from South Uist, and Bill Cruickshanks were big contributors to the New Zealand scene. So while New Zealand is so far away from Scotland there was a lot of contact with good pipers. As a nation New Zealanders are quite driven. If you look at rugby, for such a small population the All Blacks are always very hard to beat. There were a lot of good pipers, combined with a lot of good tuition so if you were keen and worked hard then the capacity existed to become quite good."

Apart from his father, Murray had two other teachers in New Zealand, and they had a huge influence on his career. "My father never had the high class tuition that he made sure I got, but he's well respected for his views on music within the piping fraternity in New Zealand. He taught me a lot about how you win and how you lose. In this game you lose a whole lot more than you win, no matter how successful you are. It just goes with the territory. He always made sure that I had good values as a winner and as a loser. He's been a big influence in many ways. Then there was Donald Bain. I was nine when I first went to Donald. He lived in the next main town north from us which was about ninety minutes away, and in the early sixties that was quite a trip. It wasn't like today when guys will fly around the globe for a weekend at a competition or a workshop. It was quite a big trek once a month to go to Donald so from age nine to age twenty there's a big time where you can learn or lose so much depending on how you deal with things. He really shaped me."

"The other option was up in Christchurch where Bill Boyle, another very famous piper, lived, or south to Allan Dodd. Both were a bit further away and so Donald was approached by dad and it couldn't really have worked out any better. He became a family friend and was more like a brother to me than a teacher. As the years went on we grew very close and he would come over from New Zealand and stay with us. He would play me a tune and ask me what I thought, and then I would play him a tune and ask what he thought. We had a really good relationship and total respect for each other. He was very proud of what I went on to achieve and I couldn't have done that without his help. When Donald came to Scotland in 1967/68 he suggested I continue with his good friend Dave Boyle, Bill's brother, who had the same principles as Donald."

It's no wonder Donald Bain was proud of the success his young student was able to forge for himself when he came to Scotland, although it's fair to say that Murray Henderson was already making a name for himself before he left New Zealand. "When I came over to Scotland in 1973 I had just won the New Zealand Championship. I had moved up through the grades quite quickly and ended up in the A Grade at fifteen, equivalent to the Open in Scotland, which was difficult because there were a lot of great players. But that was part of the challenge, to pit yourself against the best that New Zealand had to offer. When I came to Scotland I had that success behind me but that doesn't really mean anything when you get onto the bigger platform."

Murray very quickly came to understand just how much bigger the platform was in Scotland. "It was because of the sheer number of good players that are on the scene. I competed at the Edinburgh Police event four weeks after I arrived and I placed fourth in the Open March competition. I think I was more surprised than anyone. At that event the list of names, and potential winners, was endless. Coming from the New Zealand scene where you may, at a typical competition, have four world-class New Zealand players, you find yourself in the midst of the cream of Scottish players, most of whom are potential winners. When Donald Bain came to Scotland in 1967 and 1968 he used to send reel-to-reel tapes of the BBC Chanter programmes, as they were called in those days, so we were hearing some of the top players of the day. Donald MacLeod toured New Zealand in 1968 and I went to a couple of his recitals, so it didn't come as a total shock. Donald Bain had prepared me well. He told me it would be very impressive, and it was."

Although the competition was tougher than Murray was used to back home, it wasn't long before he was making a name for himself. "I had been round the games circuit in 1973 and got a few prizes here and there, but it was very difficult because unlike today most of the top players played at lots of the games. There would generally be more Gold Medallists competing than there were prizes so you knew straight away that you were there for the experience rather than a prize! But that was great as you were learning so much from listening and participating. In 1974 I won the Pìobaireachd at Nethy Bridge which was my first 'first' in Scotland. Then I won the Gold Medal for pìobaireachd at Braemar the same year and went on to win the Inverness Gold Medal in 1975, so I was starting to make my way."

In those days even the most successful solo players weren't able to make a living playing the pipes. Murray's family had been farmers in New Zealand, and that's where he started when he came to Scotland. "When I arrived I worked on a farm on the outskirts of Dundee. My family farmed in New Zealand, mostly sheep, and I would have liked to have worked on a farm that was more animal orientated but the problem with looking after animals is you don't have the flexibility to get off for piping as easily. Instead I worked on an arable farm as a tractor man. It was great and the farmer that I worked for were really understanding. I didn't take any set holidays but I gave the farmer a note of the days I wanted off for piping and that suited him. I was away for a day or two here or there so when the other workers were away for their two weeks in the summer I was there to cover, apart from days when I wanted to go to a games. I had a lot of freedom to do what I wanted."

One of the things that Murray wanted to do was make reeds. "I became a full-time reed maker in 1976 although it started as a hobby in 1974. I'd be working during the day on the farm and then when I was practicing I'd be messing around with reeds and it all got a bit ungainly, so I made the decision to go full-time in 1976. On reflection it was a big step to leave the security of my job but at the time it didn't seem like it, being young was probably an advantage. As you get older you start to ask whether you should do this or do that but when you're younger you just do it. Probably the same philosophy as I have with my piping. If you work hard enough at something you can make it a success. That was the challenge."

While there is no doubt that Murray has a great work ethic, and the discipline needed to succeed at whatever he turns his hand to, he does accept that the business he chose helped that decision. "It's a cottage industry. You don't have to think about renting or buying premises. Patricia and I were living near Glamis and had bought the old railway cottage there and used one of the rooms to work from. You just figured that if you could sell enough reeds to meet your mortgage you would be fine. We've built up an international business. It was so different then to what it is now. It would be such a big step now to give up the security of the day job, if there is such a thing these days as a day job with security."

Not that Murray associated a day job making reeds with more success in his piping endeavours. "Piping has always been such a big part of my life and it was great to be so closely involved in something that was associated with my first love. It gave Patricia and me the freedom to go for a tour round the games if we wished, bearing in mind that when we came home we had to make up that time."

Although Murray was working with reeds and pipes all day, he didn't think of it as an easy route to competition success. "I didn't believe that by making reeds all day it would help my playing. You talk to players who teach all day and they say that the last thing they feel like doing when they go home at night is to get the pipes out and practice."

But you do have to practice, and Murray has strong views on the relationship between hard work and success, and not just on the competition boards. "If you want to be good at something you have to spend a lot of time at it, it's really as simple as that. There's no doubt that there has to be something there in the first place for you to work on and bring out, but I think that there has to be a lot of scope for self-improvement. If you could be born with it then a lot of people would have it, wouldn't they? Most people are born with the capacity to be good at something if they put in the appropriate amount of time. You get the odd geniuses like John D Burgess who won the Medals at sixteen. That's not something that was taught. I think a lot of people have the ability to succeed if they would just go the extra mile. You have to be fortunate in a number of ways. The biggest thing is that you must have good tuition, and if you have that right from the word go, along with some natural talent, then you should be able to get to the top level."

"I've always travelled with the mind-set that if you're going to do something you need to put your best foot forward and give it your best shot. I didn't set out to be a successful piper. I set out to be as good a piper as I could be and I didn't know where that would take me. I'd never heard about the Gold Medals until I was fifteen so how could I have set out to win one?"

The fact that Murray has won more than one Gold Medal, along with just about every other prize in the piping world, is down in part to his belief that he has to try to be as good as he can be. In order to do that he has a methodical practice regime. "When I was in full flight competitively it would be nothing to play for two or three hours in a night. If the event was in two weeks' time I would be easing off; all of the hard work would be done. The hard work started fifty years ago. Your preparation actually starts when you begin your first lessons if you are a serious player. You build all of the foundations as you go along so that you're not going back all of the time and revisiting any issues and thinking 'Oh, I didn't learn this properly'."

Murray reckons he was fortunate that his teacher made sure that the foundations were all in place early on. "That's why I keep coming back to the fact that Donald Bain has been the most influential person on my career because he made sure that every time he taught me something he taught me correctly and I learned it correctly. So you build and you build and then you get to the stage where you're getting to Gold Medal level."

When you get to that stage, the way you organise your practice and learning becomes really important. "Back in the mid-seventies the tunes used to be announced at the Northern Meeting for the following year's event. So you would go to London to play in the Bratach Gorm then put the pipes away for a few weeks before you would start to learn the set tunes. The plan was always to have the set tunes learned for Christmas, and then you started to build them over the winter months. So my preparation for Inverness would start by learning the set tunes and I always started to learn them early."

Murray talks about 'learning' tunes and 'building' tunes, and they are not the same thing. "You can't begin to understand a tune until you have it memorised. You have to memorise it and be totally comfortable with the order of the notes. Then you start to add the musical touches. Technique should always be a given. If you're at Gold Medal level and you've been well taught from a young age there shouldn't be any technical issues. For sure technique needs to be practiced and I was never shy at practising. I used to use the practice chanter for technique and the bagpipe for playing the tunes so that I would never play pìobaireachd on the practice chanter. I would memorise it by looking at the score and singing it, and the first time that I would play the tune would be on the pipes. All of the memorisation, and getting friendly with the piece first, and only then start looking at the colour you can put into it."

The learning part shouldn't be the bit that takes the time. "You would look to memorise a tune in a night if you had two or three yours you could dedicate to it. If not, you would certainly break the back of it and endorse it the next day. The style I use is to learn the tune by singing so there is a lot of time in the day when you can run through variations. You don't have to have your practice chanter, just find a quiet corner and sing it. I would do a lot of thinking about the tune and how I could shape it and the colours I could put in. Then you should play it on the pipes, record it and listen to it, or go to your lesson and get feedback. Keep it going until both teacher and pupil are happy."

Although you never are really happy, according to Murray. "There are always things that you can improve. I don't think you really understand a tune until you've played it for two or three years and then let it go and come back to it. If you're learning a lot of tunes it's impossible to keep them all going. If you have a dozen or fifteen tunes each year that you are working on you can come back to them and you'll see something else in it that you maybe didn't see before."

It was always going to be the case that you like some of the set tunes more than others, and Murray developed a way of dealing with that as well. "I've spent a lifetime learning set tunes that I'm not necessarily fond of at all but you just have to learn them. I always made sure that whatever the set tune requirement was I would learn more so that I could throw away the unattractive ones. All you were doing was going through a process of telling yourself that you had rejected a few tunes rather than telling yourself 'don't fancy this, don't fancy that and I don't really like this but I'll need to learn it because I have to have six tunes'. There was always something comforting knowing that you might be left with a tune you didn't really want but that you had rejected others that were less appealing to get there."

It is also the case that from time to time tunes will grow on you. "Sometimes you'll see things in tunes after a while that you didn't see on your first look at it. The skill then becomes finding something in it, or bringing something out of it."

Murray also reckons that you can't just turn up on the day, hope for the best, and expect to play a good tune. "I'd play each one for months before the competition. I know some pipers are able to play the tune for the first time on the day of the competition but I need to be in the comfort zone. The idea is that if you are trying to perform a piece rather than just trying to play it with the right notes, you have to be really comfortable with it. Over the long haul the players who have been successful are generally the ones that have put a lot of hard work into the tunes."

This adage applies equally to the instrument as well as the tunes. "You spend time on the instrument and you should never be satisfied with anything less than perfection. That's why you're never satisfied. It's easier these days with the equipment that we have. The people with really good instruments still work really hard, and that's why their instrument sounds slightly better than the average. That will be why their technique, or their musical interpretation, will be better than the average, because they work harder at everything. It's about trying to create a package and it's all a discipline."

It's a discipline that Murray Henderson has worked hard at maintaining over the years. As well as being taught in his early years by his father and Donald Bain, he cites another couple of influences that helped his playing. "Bob Nicol was great when I came to Scotland. That was a different relationship because I very much saw myself as the little boy and he was the schoolmaster. It was different from my relationship with Donald Bain. Bob taught me from when I arrived here until his death in 1978. Jimmie McGregor helped me through three of my Glenfiddich Championships and that was a different take on things. For example, I'd always been taught that the first beat in the bar is very precious in two-four marches, and you must always make sure it is the stronger of the two. Jimmy introduced me to the off-beat and that was a whole new world to me."

"My wife Patricia has also been a great help, particularly over the past twenty odd years. I would always ask her advice on how my tunes were coming across, as she has a fantastic appreciation of the qualities that make up a good performance. She was a tremendous support over my competitive career".

Murray Henderson was open to advice from all quarters, and he had no doubt that this helped as well. "When I arrived here in 1973 I was all eyes and ears and you learn a lot from the senior competitors of the day, the household names. You competed against them at the Games and some indoor competitions, then you observed them in the Clasp, for instance, until you were lucky enough to play against them in the elite events and their whole professionalism was great. You learn what not to do as well as what you should do, and they were all easy to approach. If you asked them what their routine was they were happy to talk and give you the benefit of their knowledge."

Whilst that might be true for the pipers Murray was competing against, the same couldn't be said for the judges, and Murray feels that this is one area where much progress has been made. Forty years ago, apart from a few ex-competitors, the judging panel was made up of a ragbag of piping scholars, landowners, colonels and lawyers. "Today's judges are pretty much now all ex-competitors. That's great because you know they have been on the boards and earned their colours. The other big difference is that you can socialise with judges these days because you feel comfortable doing that. Forty years ago as a twenty-year-old lad fresh off the boat from New Zealand it wouldn't have crossed my mind to approach a bench and ask them what they thought of my tune. It just wasn't the thing to do. Maybe some of the senior players did. Maybe Hugh McCallum or Iain MacFadyen did speak to DR McLellan or Frank Richardson and ask them what they thought. Now it's nothing for a junior player to speak to a senior judge and ask for an opinion. There is no divide and that's fantastic. It's likely that you might get a crit sheet now, and that's something you wouldn't have got, even thirty years ago."

Technology has also helped to make the piping world a smaller place. "The fact that there is so much access to material on the net, and so much access to tuition the world over, means that the piping world has got a lot smaller and is extremely healthy. There are more people striving to be better players, and that's possibly because the numbers are greater, but there are also a lot of people trying very hard. Forty years ago, at Gold Medal level, you might have thought that if you had a steady sound and played a decent tune you wouldn't be too far away. Now if you don't have that then you don't even get started. The expectation of performance has got higher which is fantastic for the overall standard. The sheer volume of competitors who want to compete at Oban and Inverness shows you how healthy things are."

Jack Lee

Jack Lee believes that the piping world, which he feels is already as healthy as it has ever been, is set for further expansion. "I see one big wave coming, and that's the American piper. I'm from Canada and I travel a lot in the USA and one thing I've learned over the years is never count that country out. There's a determination in the US and there's a tremendous growth in piping. There's a big increase in fire-fighter pipe bands, police pipe bands and piping in general. I could see at some point a lot of big players coming from the USA and it would not surprise me in my lifetime if the World Championship was won by an American pipe band. They have quality players. There have been great players like Mike Cusack, who is the greatest of all the American pipers. It's getting better and better and I think there is a future wave of pipers to come from the US. If you add these Eastern States together — Massachusetts, New Jersey, Pennsylvania and New York, then you have a number of pipers far greater than those playing in Scotland. These guys are playing in three or four bands and having fun. They're not worrying too much about the quality and they're not aspiring to be professional pipers but they're enjoying it, and I think that should always be a really big part of it."

There has been a vibrant piping scene in North America for decades. "I have a theory as to why there are so many pipers over here. This continent was settled by people from many lands but the Irish and Scottish immigrants formed a big part of the culture in North America. When they came to this part of the world they brought their culture with them. A higher percentage of Scots came to Canada and a higher percentage of the Irish went to the United States, so you'll see a tremendous Irish community throughout their country and you'll see a big proud Scottish community coast to coast in Canada. Long before I came along the British Columbia Pipers Association was operating very strongly in this area and their mission was simply to foster piping in this part of the world. They did a great job of that and when they had their annual gatherings they would bring out the top Scottish players to do recitals and teach. In the early days it was a solo piping culture and then the bands became much more popular in the sixties and seventies. Now in this part of the world pipe bands are very prominent and are a very big part of the Scottish community. There is still an emphasis on good quality solo playing and we have a very vibrant community of Highland games and Piobaireachd Clubs. All kinds of things which will encourage good solo playing."

There is no question that Jack Lee was part of that tradition even before he picked up a chanter. "I was very fortunate to be born into a piping family. My great grandfather was a piper and he learned from Keith Cameron, son of Donald Cameron. I had a number of pipers in the family, and my uncle was very connected with a lot of friends in the piping community so I always had a chance to be around good pipers. In the sixties it was the early days of piping schools in North America and a lot of the great pipers were coming over here, Seumas MacNeill, Captain John MacLellan, Bob Hardie, Andrew Wright, and Donald MacLeod, so I had the opportunity to take instruction from some Scottish piping legends. My uncle, my brother Terry, and I connected with the top teacher Jimmy McMillan. We had great fun taking lessons from Jimmy. He was always emphasising good playing."

Although Jack has always been a piper, his brother Terry, now pipe major of Simon Fraser University Pipe Band, started life as a highland dancer. "Terry won the Braemar Shield three times and when he won it for the first time the Royal Family was there. It was a male only competition in those days, maybe 1969 or 1970, and there was a concern amongst the local population because it had never gone to a non-Scot before. They would not allow the Queen to present the trophy to Terry because he was from Canada. Prince Phillip and Terry met behind the outhouse so that they could shake hands and the Prince could give Terry the Braemar Shield. When we came back to Canada some people in our community heard about this and they got very motivated to send Terry back to Scotland. He went back and went on to win the Shield again, and this time the Queen did present the trophy. My mother has a wonderful photo on her wall of the Queen shaking hands with Terry and all the little Princes are also in the photo. On that particular trip I came over as well and competed in the amateurs, picking a few prizes here and there at Cowal and Braemar. I'd have been fifteen at the time."

For Jack Lee it was the start of a love affair with Scotland that has lasted nearly forty years, and counting. "I've been to Scotland almost one hundred times. I've been pretty much every year, often three or four times. I just love to play there and I especially love it when I feel that I'm playing well. I look forward to going every year. When I was eighteen I was pipe major of a Grade 2 band called Canadian Pacific Airlines. It was a good strong Grade 2 band for those days and we actually won first at Cowal and the Scottish

Championship at Rothesay. That was in 1976 and it was also the first time I had played solos as an open player. I played at Oban, and although I wasn't the strongest player I made the finals of the light music and was very happy with that."

As well as the opportunity to play in Scotland, those early visits gave Jack the opportunity to listen to players he had only ever read about. "I heard Pipe Major Angus MacDonald, Dr Angus MacDonald and Bill Livingstone, all pipers that I had never heard up close and it was really exciting for me. The next time I came back was 1978 and I went to the Northern Meetings at Inverness. I had a grand week and I ended up winning two firsts in the light music — the March and the Strathspey and Reel were separate events — and I got a third in the Silver Medal. Based on that I got into the Gold Medal competition after that and also into the Former Winners so that was when I really got the bug to come over and compete."

It was a much harder world to be part of in those days. "I remember there were seventy-nine players in the Inverness March, eighty-one in the Strathspey and Reel, and it went on and on all day. It was really tough on the judges. That was one of the last years before they split it into an A and B class. There were just so many players, and so many really good players. In Canada there would have been around fifteen to twenty competing in comparable events."

In those early days Jack was trying to juggle full-time work with his piping, and it didn't make for an easy life. "I was working as an accountant and I had a wife and children. It was very difficult to find the time. I always thought that someday it would get better but in fact it never has and it's never easy to find the time to play the way I would like to. It's always been about a few minutes here and a few minutes there. Sometimes I'm practicing late at night and at others it's early in the morning. For about ten years I worked for a major oil company as a supervisor of a group of accountants at Chevron. I had my personal key to the storage locker and that would let me go down at lunchtime. That was the only way I could practice because I was leaving the house at six in the morning and getting home at five-thirty at night. There was never much time."

Jack is very fortunate that his family have the same hobby as him. "My wife and I have three children, Andrew, Colin and John. They are all professional level pipers who are involved in solo playing and who play in Scotland. They all play in SFU so they have reached a level of playing where they travel with me. I have often thought that if my children had taken up another hobby then I would not have been quite so involved in piping because I would have been involved with them in whatever they chose to do.

They came with me to the Highland games when they were young, caught the bug, and learned how to play so that was very helpful."

Jack is one of a handful of top players who has managed to combine a successful career in solo competition with success in one of the most prolific prize winning bands in history. He believes that they feed off each other. "To me there is not a great deal of difference in the music between top solo playing and top band playing. We play in the SFU band and consider ourselves to be a very expressive band. We play with solo expression and always try to make sure that the quality of playing is very high in the band with good attention to detail. We definitely try to do that in solos, so although I have to spend more time playing because I have an involvement in both, I believe that one helps the other. Playing in the band helps my solo work and being a committed solo player helps the band."

It's all made a bit easier now, not just because Jack's family are involved in the piping world, but also because he has managed to turn his piping into a business as well as his hobby. "I was getting invited all over the place to do things and I had to say no much more often than I was saying yes because I just didn't have the vacation time. Being an accountant, it took me a while to think about it and crunch some numbers. Another thing that was a factor for me was that we had two pipers in our band killed in a car accident, Robert and Malcolm. Now I live by the 'life is short' principle."

"When I worked for Chevron we would get memos telling us that people had passed away and often it was just after they had retired. I always thought that it was really sad to work all these years for a company and then not get a chance to enjoy retirement. These things had an impact on me. We now have our own family business, Lee & Son Bagpipes, and we manufacture pipe bags and reeds. I'm super busy with that and I travel a lot doing workshops all over North America. I Skype a lot, I have a number of Skype students around the world, and I run a big piping school out here in the summer time. I am so glad that I made the switch to full-time piping."

Skype is a relatively new addition to the piping teacher's arsenal and there are differences between Skype and face-to-face teaching. "There are things you can do well on Skype and things you can't do so well. You can critique a person's fingering and technique. There is also a little less banter and socialising using Skype, and the students love that part. When we were children going to Jimmy MacMillan for lessons we would leave the house for six, get there for seven, have a lesson until eight, and get home for nine. A three-hour commitment for a one hour lesson. Now the student clicks a button at seven and goes at eight. What you can't do is help them with the tuning so much, and you can't blow their pipes for them to see if they're going well or if they're having any problems. I try to work around that as much as I can. I have a number of students that I do see during the year and I help with the instrument, or if they are Skype students who play in pipe bands, then their pipe major can help with their instrument. Skype is great for pipers who don't have access to good regular instruction and there are a number of teachers around the world doing what I do."

Skype also helps some of the players in Simon Fraser University Pipe Band who don't live in the Vancouver area. "We've become a destination band. People love to come from a long way away to play with us. They have to be very strong players to do that because the bar is so high. They have to know the tunes, the instrument has to be going well, and they have to blend in right away. For some of these guys it's a great set-up because they don't have to go to band practice twice a week. They Skype in once in a while, they work on their tunes, and they fly themselves in so they can spend a much shorter time playing in a pipe band, yet they can come in and play at a very high level with a band like SFU. It's great for them and it's great for us. We have strong players in the band but it's always better to have great players from all over the world who want to come and play with us and help take us over the bar just a little bit. We split the cost with them and try to support them. We have people applying every year to get in to the band but it's pretty tough."

It's not just tough for the players from overseas to get into SFU, locals find there is a lot of competition for places in the band. "We turn down a lot from Vancouver. We just don't have enough room. We also have a very vibrant junior band, Robert Malcolm Memorial, and one of the principles is that we don't hold anyone back. If their playing is strong they can go from the Grade 4 band to the Grade 2 band. If their playing is really strong then we try to give them an opportunity in the Grade 1 band, so players are continually flowing through. We've had the RMM band going for twenty years now and still only a small percentage of players actually make it to SFU. By the time they get to that level of playing they are busy with university or their personal lives, and so we run the RMM band not for the specific role of providing payers for SFU. We run the RMM band because we enjoy teaching kids. We have kids coming in the door pretty regularly and it's fun to teach them and see how far they can go with their piping and drumming."

They can go as far as they like, would seem to be the answer, and for the players in the SFU band, and Jack Lee, that means regular trips to Scotland for competition. It's become big business for the band, and it's an expensive business. "Fortunately for me the majority of trips I've made have been funded by someone else. In the early days the pipe band would fly us over and then I got a number of trips by winning prizes over here. If I come to Glenfiddich then they pay for the trip. It varies, and different pipe bands have flown me over to help tune them up and get them ready for competition, so there haven't been too many times that I've had to pay myself."

"As far as the band is concerned it is getting more expensive. Flights are costing more every year, although the flight is not the most significant part of the cost; it's the cost of living when we get there. We are always pretty amazed at how short a distance our dollar will go in Scotland where things are very expensive and so it's a matter of budgeting and saving. The band is supported by Simon Fraser University, a major University in Canada with Scottish heritage, and we are part of the fabric of the University. They are proud of the pipe band, in fact they have just awarded Terry and me Honorary Doctorates, and they support us a bit."

"We raise a lot of our money through concert performance and the sale of CDs, T-shirts, baseball caps and the like, at events and through our website. We try to keep the cost down by staying in university dormitories and those sorts of things. We've been every year for 30 years, and some years we've been two or three times, so it's a big undertaking, but it's part of what the band is. People join the band because it is going to Scotland and playing at a very high level and it's part of the expectation of players who join the band. I'm sure we hold the record for the amount of money that any pipe band in history has ever spent going to Scotland."

Although Jack, and everyone else in the band, loves their trips to Scotland, he believes that they shouldn't have to come so often. "It's very difficult to understand why the World Championships should always be in Scotland when it's the 'world' championship. It's hard to find one other global cultural or sporting event where the World Championship is always in the same country. That seems like something that needs to be changed. The next move should be New York or Toronto, it's a World Championship and world should mean world not just Scotland, even though the Scots are brilliant at hosting it. It should go back to Scotland every fourth year or something."

That's not the only change Jack wants to see. "There are far too few judges, and the impact that one drumming or ensemble judge can have on the result is just staggering. In most events you need a panel of judges, you throw out the high scores, you throw out the low, you take the ones in the middle, and juggle them a bit."

Although Jack wants to see more judges in the pipe band arena, he won't count himself among that bigger panel when he puts away his pipes. "I would judge solo competitions but not bands. I'm inspired by Jim McGillivray in this. He's a Clasp winner and a great piper. He went down the pipe band judging path and it was so discouraging for him, so many hurdles to overcome, and then maybe every fourth year, if you are lucky and your name is on the list, you can hope for a Grade 1 circle. Every other year becomes tougher and less enjoyable. Then he got into solo judging and in year one he's judging the Gold Medal, year two the Clasp, year three the Silver Medal and Former Winners March, Strathspey and Reel, and he's having so much fun listening to top players at their best. It was just a much more pleasant experience. So I can see myself really enjoying judging solos (as long as my children are not competing because I would never judge them) and I think I could be a really good judge. However, the way it is set up in the pipe band world I can't see myself becoming a pipe band judge."

Jack believes that you have to have certain qualities to judge solo competition. "I think that the players have earned the right to be judged by their peers. So when you are playing at Gold Medal and Clasp level then I like to see judges who have achieved that level of competence on the instrument. They don't have to have won the Clasp to judge it but they do have to have been playing at that level. I would bring that to the table. I'm open minded and not absolutely entrenched in one style or another. I think great music is great music and I love to hear other interpretations of old classic tunes. I have a lot of experience because I have been competing at the top level for more than thirty years and I think I would enjoy and do a good job as a solo judge."

During the thirty years that he has been competing Jack has seen many changes. "The number one enhancement in piping over the last thirty years has been the ability to manage moisture in the instrument. It started out with water traps, seasoning, synthetic bags, synthetic drone reeds, silica gel, crystals inside the bag and all these things to manage the moisture so that the chance to hear an instrument go wildly out of tune is much lower now than it used to be. The ability to sway the contest in a positive direction by having a great instrument is a lot less. People used to talk about the legendary instrument of Donald MacPherson and in my opinion it was true. He would hypnotise you with those drones, they were absolutely breathtaking. Donald did so well because in addition to being a great piper he had an instrument that was clearly better than anyone else that I had heard at that point. That ability to have such an advantage is pretty much gone today."

Although impressed with Donald MacPherson's sound, Jack believes that the tone of the pipes comes from the player as much as from the instrument. "I think bagpipe tone comes from the internal ear and I think that a good piper will take the tone that his ear tells him to take and Donald just knew what he wanted. He wouldn't settle for second best, and he knew the harmonics of the drone and how they blended together with the rich chanter sound that he had. It was fantastic and it was a game changer."

As well as delivering the right sound from the bagpipe, the other thing that Jack Lee believes you have to deliver is consistency, but he also thinks it is like chasing an impossible dream. "No one is completely consistent. I've been doing this at the top level for thirty years and I've had some highs and lows. I have three personal traits that have helped me. I'm a very determined person when I want to do something. I just try to do it and try to get over the hurdles. There is always stuff coming at you that will stop you doing the things you really want to do but I just try to get over it. The second thing is that I have an ability to bounce back. I tell my students this all the time. When you're down, it's not the fact that you're down that's important, it's how fast you get back up that counts. So I do try to get back up quickly and I never stay down for long. The third thing I have is a very thick skin. If you don't have a thick skin you'll not last in this business. You will be finished."

Then there is the ability to deal with your nerves. "It's very much a mental game. Essentially when you are on stage at a major event you are not yourself. The effects of nerves have hit you and you have less of your memory available, less of your mental capacity. Any sensitivity in the instrument seems to magnify itself. It's very important to just settle down on stage and catch a moment. Play a wee bit, tune the bagpipe, calm yourself down, and get yourself back to where you need and want to be before you start. Part of it is about warming the instrument, but for me a big part of it is just calming myself down and getting back to where I was and as close as I can to when I was practising at home. I used to marvel at Alasdair Gillies; it seemed that he had nerves of steel. Willie McCallum too. When he's going well, he might think inside that something might go wrong but as a listener I don't get that feeling. I think it's just fantastic when he's in the zone. I suppose we all have moments like that when we are in the right zone. As you approach the end of a performance it's probably natural to have thoughts like 'don't screw up, let's just get to the finish line'. I try not to think about stuff like that."

Jack's ability to shut these images out has obviously worked over the years and his hundred or so visits to Scotland have brought him an incredible haul of prizes, both at band and individual level. Although he has had great satisfaction from every one of them he is keen to point out that it's not only winning that keeps him going. "The most excited I ever got was SFU winning its first World Championship. Then there was my first Gold Medal at Inverness in 1981. These are the two that really stand out. Others would be The Glenfiddich and the Silver Stars at Inverness. For me though it's not about the prize, it's about the journey. I love to take my playing to another level and always try to play my best. I feel that if someone beats me, which is often the case, then as long as I play well I feel really good about it. I'm not prize driven, I'm performance driven and for me it must be a good performance or it's very discouraging."

Although it's about performance not prizes for Jack, he's more than happy with his trophy cabinet. "There is not one prize that I haven't won that I need to win. I've won all of the prizes I could ever hope to and I kind of feel that if any more come my way it's gravy on top. It would be great to win again and I would love it but if I hang up my pipes today I'd walk away very satisfied with my career."

Jack has no intention of hanging up his pipes in the near future but he does admit that this is one of the questions he is asked regularly, along with whether he would give up the band or the solo playing if forced to make a choice. "Murray Henderson was very inspiring, but now that he has retired that makes me the old guy. The honest answer is that I don't know when I'll retire. I keep thinking that at some point my body will tell me it's time, that it won't be able to do things that I want to do, but it hasn't quite happened yet. As for the second question, I love both. I love playing pìobaireachd when the pipes are going well and you're into a great tune, but I love it when the band is going well and we're heading toward the Worlds."

The other important thing for Jack is that he'll keep playing, solo and with the band, as long as he's enjoying himself. "It needs to be about fun. It's a hobby and a passion, and we love doing it. I think piping done well is every bit as fun as playing baseball or football or tennis. It's a fantastic hobby for a young person and I tell the kids in the Robert Malcolm Memorial Band that all the time. Take time to enjoy it and get as much out of it as you can. You'll get as much out of it as you put into it so take lessons, get going, and have a ball playing the bagpipes. These are very exciting times."

Willie McCallum

There is an on-going argument in the piping community about the length of time taken by competitors tuning their pipes at competitions. There are those who say that the time allocated for tuning on the boards should be strictly limited while others argue that the competitors need the time to get settled before they start their tune, particularly in pìobaireachd competitions. For Willie McCallum it's not clear-cut. "Tuning is fifty percent about the pipes and fifty percent about the piper. You know that you have to do two things. You have to have the pipes at their optimum for you, but you do know that this will come in time. A lot of it is about going through the process knowing that you will need a few minutes to regulate the temperature and the humidity. The rest of it is just about going through what you're going to do and what you're going to play in your head and to get a level of comfort with the surroundings."

Willie usually has a level of comfort with his pipes, and so for him the time spent tuning is more of a mental issue. "I know that the pipes are going to be fine in time, if you don't think they're going to be fine then you probably shouldn't be up there, so it's just a case of playing the pipes, and playing a couple of things that settle you down. You're bound to be nervous when you blow the pipes up on stage. It doesn't matter how many times you've done it, you don't get any less nervous. You maybe just learn to deal with it better. I try to make sure that I'm comfortable with what I'm doing and that I have prepared well. If you have the confidence to know that you have prepared well then it will help you through the nervous bits of your performance. Even when you start and you think everything is nice and calm, it's amazing what happens up there in the middle of a tune. It's about keeping the faith in what you've done and the practice you've put in so that when you come to a wee nervous bit the preparation and knowledge kicks in.

The preparation and knowledge don't just kick in when things go wrong. "It could be nerves because it's a difficult part of the tune or it could be because things are going so well and you start to realise that the pipes are really locked in and you're playing as well as you have been all year, and that can make it worse, because you suddenly start to think that it's all there. Some days it's not, some days it's really hard work, but when everything is working that can make it worse and can make you more nervous."

There is an adrenalin rush to being on the platform, and Willie has felt it since the day he started to compete. "I love competition and the buzz I get from that is hard to beat. It could be almost like a sport if you let it. For me it's about trying to be the best I can be on the day. I treat every competition in the same way, whether it's The Glenfiddich or a smaller one. It's always been about getting me to a place where I can be absolutely on my game. Even in the juniors I practiced a lot so that I could play as well as possible and it's a hunger to be that way. It's not so much that you're doing it to win, you do want to win of course, but the motivation is in wanting to play well."

That hunger will tell Willie when it's time to hang up his pipes. "I think when I get to the stage that I can't motivate myself to be like that, or I don't have the time to do it, or just don't enjoy it, that would be the time where I would stop competing. The other thing is that I want to always be good enough to win. Whether I win or not is another thing, but to know that my standard is good enough to have a chance to win is where my judgement call would be, it's all about the performance."

While there is a hunger to do well and to win, Willie also gets great enjoyment being around all of his fellow competitors throughout the competition season. "It's amazing that the people I have been competing against for twenty or twenty-five years are all friendly and we all get on really well on the day. Some of that is just about having a laugh together and that helps the whole situation and helps to ease the tension on the day. I kind of look forward to that now. If I didn't have that relationship with the guys it might take some of the enjoyment out of it. It's quite a big social thing and that's an important part of it all. If we all stayed in our tuning rooms and didn't talk to each other then it wouldn't be much fun. I hope it will never be different to the way it is now."

It's always been like that for Willie McCallum. He is very much part of the inner circle of competitors today but he was impressed by the way the then inner circle helped him when he was a novice. "When I saw the older guys competing when I was younger they were all very friendly. I'm thinking of Hugh McCallum, Duncan and Iain MacFadyen, Angus MacDonald and John McDougall. All these guys got on well with each other and I think it's a great thing for piping the way that works; it's not win at all costs. They were all friendly to me when I started. They were very encouraging and when I got into the bigger competitions it was really quite hard to grasp that I was actually playing against my heroes. It took me a while to get the hang of that."

Now that Willie is one of the most established players of his generation he has started thinking about who will come after him, and how they will compare. "From the current generation there are a few great prospects. In the light music Finlay Johnston is a very good player with a huge future, Calum Beaumont as well. They're two of the rising stars. Then you have Andrew Carlisle, they're all beating on the door and have done really well in big competition. There are others that are nearly there and have a lot of ability. There are more young people playing than when I was young."

Are they any better than Willie and his compatriots? "Certainly the standard of the instrument is better than it was but I'm not sure if the players are any better. Although there are a few excellent young players, I wouldn't say that any generation is better than another. I couldn't imagine that any generation could be better than the one before us which had the likes of John Burgess, Iain MacFadyen, Donald MacPherson, Hugh McCallum, John McDougall, Ian Morrison and all these guys. Every generation has great players. We've been fortunate that there has been a group of us that have been there for ever as far as some people are concerned but that will happen with the next generation as well."

Willie was groomed for a life as a piper from a very young age, and accepts that it was inevitable he would play. "I come from a family with generation after generation of pipers and I was exposed to it in a big way. My father was particularly keen. He played when he was younger, although not too much after the age of eighteen. All the brothers in the house played to different degrees. Three of them turned out to be very good pipers, Hugh being the most famous. He went on to win many major competitions several times over."

"My first teacher was my dad's brother Ronald. He was a very good light music player and he was pipe major of the local band in Campbeltown when I was a wee boy. He was a very good player. He taught Ronnie McShannon amongst others, so that's where I started. My dad showed me the scale, and a couple of other things, then it was off to Ronald to get moving on. There was another brother, Archie, who was a very successful competitor but he was killed at nineteen in a hit and run accident on his bike. Hugh was born after Archie died and Hugh's pipes are the ones that Archie played. The pipes I play were Ronald's pipes. Just as I was starting to get on the pipes I had a loan of a set, but then Ronnie retired and I inherited the silver pipes that my grandfather had bought. I play them in competitions and they're the ones that I've won ninety-nine percent of my prizes on."

Willie knows that he is very lucky to have inherited these pipes. "Lots of people go through a long search for pipes. The ones that I started to play at the age of eleven are an old set of Hendersons made in the 1890s. They have been in the family for seventy or eighty years. They were sold to my grandfather by an old chap called Willie Thompson. He was an Aberdeenshire man who came down to work with the MacNeils in Kintyre as a gardener and he taught a lot of famous pipers, including Pipe Major Ronnie McCallum MBE, who was a cousin of my father. He was also Stuart Liddell's grandfather, so it's all the same family. He taught John Wilson's father as well, so Willie was responsible for a lot of teaching. He also taught John MacKenzie and he had a really big input in Kintyre. The pipes that I have, the pipes that Hugh has, and the pipes that Ronnie McShannon has, were all bought from Willie Thomson."

Little did Willie know when he started playing - largely because it wasn't the done thing at that time - that he would end up playing and teaching music full-time. That is where he finds himself now, dividing his time between a heavy competing schedule and an even heavier teaching schedule that takes him all over the world, particularly to the USA. "I think it's a big cultural thing with both the Irish and Scottish communities in New York. I believe there are more pipers in New York than there are in Scotland and the number of pipe bands is huge. All of the police and fire departments have their own bands. They kind of mix and match as well because some of them play in more than one. I was talking to a guy recently who played in his own band and four others. They do this to help make up the numbers for parades and stuff."

How does the standard compare to what he finds back in Scotland? "The standard varies, some are very good players and there are others who will just learn a few tunes and enjoy going out to the parades. These bands need bodies and there can be a rush to get them out there to play. Some of them will tell us, when they come to the summer schools, that they were being fast tracked into the band when they maybe shouldn't have been. They come to the extra schools and we teach to take a step back and get on a different programme to play better."

The schools aren't restricted to the USA. Willie is a regular instructor at the busy circuit of schools that take place all year round now in Germany. "I have a number of individual students who I teach regularly; sometimes by Skype, sometimes they come here, and sometimes I go there. It just depends. The most recent one I attended was aimed at a number of pretty good players over there and they have put together a package that allows me to get my fee for doing the school, so I'm happy with that."

"They prefer to get two or three days of really concentrated stuff to help them progress. I see most of them maybe two out of every three or four weeks on Skype and I'm maybe over there every couple of months. I work with a band out there and sometimes I'll go an extra day and meet up with the people I teach and that helps with a bit of extra money to fund the trip, but it's good to be regular with them. There is a lot of talent there, and a range of abilities. There are a lot of talented people who don't have huge amount of time and perhaps are not as good as they could be. But it's the same here."

It's not easy making a living as a piping instructor these days, and Willie believes that every little helps when it comes to fitting in as many lessons as possible when he teaches overseas. This is so different from the way things were done when Willie was growing up, when money very rarely changed hands between teacher and pupil. "People used to do it in their spare time, and with me it was family, so maybe that was a bit different. Nowadays people are seeing that there are a lot more professionals teaching full-time and they need to make a living, so that is certainly part of it. It has improved the quality of the teaching and will, in some cases, improve the commitment from the students because they are paying for it. I think that might be the biggest thing about it."

Although Willie reckons that the fact students are paying for lessons does make them more motivated to learn, there are occasions where progress isn't what it should be. "How do you motivate a student who is not working? I tend to say to them that we could have a bigger gap between lessons and that would give them more time to prepare. Quite often they will volunteer this. I mean life is busy for most people and you can understand that. Sometimes we'll just have a short lesson and then we'll leave it for two weeks so that they have time to practice and get to know the music, because you don't learn it by doing nothing. Most of the time they are honest enough and say that they haven't had time, but often I'll hear it in their playing and ask them if they need more time to practice."

"Sometimes you know there is no point, unless there is a plan. You don't like to be paid when you're not helping. Personally, I like to know that there is something coming out of the lesson for the student. You get satisfaction when you hear people progress and you see them making a breakthrough that they have worked at themselves and they come to you and ask if they are doing something right. The test is that if they didn't feel they were progressing they would soon get fed up and look for some other avenue. The fact that they keep coming back gives you the satisfaction that you're doing something right."

Willie McCallum used to spend his days working as an accountant and fit his piping into weekends and evenings. He feels that the extra time he devotes to piping now has improved the quality of his playing because he has more time to prepare, not because he spends any more time practicing. "I'm usually a one practice person and normally do a solid forty or fifty minutes on the pipes every day. I wouldn't normally do much more than that unless there was something special happening or I was tinkering with the pipes. I try to make the effort for that time with the pipes going well."

"The weekend before a major competition is where the hard work starts. On the Saturday and Sunday I'll do my normal practice and then I'll do another top-up later in the day, usually half an hour. I wouldn't play longer in one stretch; instead I'll have a second practice. On the Saturday I'll try to do all of my light music really intensely and most of the big competitions will either have a MSR twice through or two tunes in each discipline, so I'm certainly working on all of those tunes and making sure I can get through them all the right number of times. That builds confidence and it builds rhythm for the whole thing. Concentration is important as well, and it's all part of the gearing up process. On top of all that, I'll also be playing my pìobaireachd so I'll be doing at least two of them every day. It takes time to do all of that and that's why I need the extra time that week. It's all about building concentration and making sure that your instrument is perfect or at least as good as you can get it. I'll have a plan for the week of what I'll be doing each day in my mind, and if I have a bit of time and things are going well I might do an extra wee bit."

Willie can't concentrate on the music he's practicing if his instrument is not set up correctly, so this is a huge issue for him. "The instrument is the main thing and if it's not right then it does disturb your concentration. There are two things; the first is that if it's not right you can't concentrate on the tune, and the second is that you know it needs to be right by the weekend and there is no getting away from that. The instrument needs to be top notch. There is nobody playing these days with a bad instrument. There are levels of good but there is no bad."

Have the levels of good changed since Willie started playing? "The instrument is the same but the set-up is completely different. When I started there was no concept of anything other than a sheepskin bag with seasoning in it and cane drone reeds. That is what I was playing up to the mid-90s. Then I changed to a couple of synthetic tenor drone reeds in about 1995 and by the end of that decade I was looking at an alternative to sheepskin because moisture was becoming an issue for me and I wanted to keep the instrument rock steady. I ended up with a synthetic bag with a moisture control system and I still use that because of the stability and consistency it gives me. Currently I use a full set of plastic drone reeds, so you could say that apart from the actual instrument itself everything that goes into it is completely different, although obviously the chanter reed is still cane. I think when I started to compete the pitch was a bit lower than it is now, but from the mid to late-80s the pitch I'm playing now won't be that far away from what I was playing then. That's important for me. I know that the pipe band pitch has been creeping up all of the time, but for the solo instrument the balance with the chanter and drones is important. If the pitch goes up too much it does something to the drones. It tends to make them quieter and you don't get the same harmonics out of them. There is a limit to where that pitch goes with the solo instrument. With the band you don't tend to get it so much, and with them it's all about getting a drone sound, and so they will adapt and select a certain type of drone reed that works at the pitch that you want to play at."

Although Willie is best known as a solo player, he did flirt with bands for a while. "The pipe band world has a completely different mentality but I did enjoy it. Not only did I play in a good band with some really great players, but both the Renfrew band and the British Caledonian Airways band had some of the best solo players. Harry McNulty was pipe major at British Caledonian Airways. The travel stuff was coming to an end when I joined the band but Harry was a great character and it took someone like him to somehow marshal the resources he had. There were a lot of really great players and I think that if it wasn't for him the whole thing could have fallen apart. The one thing about Harry was that every person in the band respected him. He was the boss. There were no egos saying what about this or what about that. Whatever he wanted you to do, you did. That takes a special type of personality."

Willie returned to the pipe band world recently to join in the adventure that was The Spirit of Scotland Pipe Band. "We never had the chance to have egos in the Spirit of Scotland Band either; we didn't have the time to work on the material and tunes we had to learn, never mind have the time to have an ego. That was another example of the need for leadership from Roddy MacLeod. It was a great experience. I'll never forget that whole week, the craic, the hard work, and the fun was great. If I hadn't done it I would have missed out on a huge experience."

A Piper's Tale

The craic and the fun come out in everything that Willie says when he talks about his piping career. He takes great delight in recounting a story of a time he spent in America with Angus McColl and Fred Morrison. "Fred and Angus and I were at a workshop in Kansas, and that's where Fred's great tune 'The Kansas City Hornpipe' came from. We got delayed and ended up in a hotel in Newark. I got woken up at 2.30am with someone knocking at my door and shouting that he needed help. Being a bit paranoid I hid the pipes on top of the wardrobe before I opened the door in case I was getting robbed, but it turned out there was a woman in a room nearby having an asthma attack. She subsequently died and I was asked the next day by detectives what I had seen and heard."

"We were all ready to go into New York the next day because we were stuck due to bad weather but as I went to leave the room there was a detective outside. He asked what I'd heard then asked what I was doing there. I told him I had been playing the pipes and was there with Fred and Angus, and he said, 'No shit, my sergeant plays'. So I answered his questions, and we were downstairs about to go into the city, when we realised the hotel was crowded with police. It turned out there had been another death at the hotel. Then a detective came running after us and told us not to go anywhere yet because the sergeant wanted to see us. The sergeant came over to talk to us. He was on the phone to a colleague of his, another piper, saying 'You'll never guess who I'm with', so he gave me the phone and I ended up talking to him. Then they wanted photos, and the poor crime scene girl, who was up to her ears in blood, had to come and take photos of this guy with Fred, Angus and me. Somewhere there is a whole photo album of dead bodies and the three of us grinning away. Then he offered us a lift into town, put the blues and twos on, and took us into the city with no time wasted! You couldn't make it up."

Finlay MacDonald

Finlay MacDonald reckons that one big thing the degree course at the Royal Conservatoire of Scotland has done is to help bring the bagpipe into the mainstream of Scottish music. "Until the late sixties pipers were not considered part of the general music scene. It was a kitsch thing on its own, and I think it was because of the military connotations. If you were a piper you made a lot of noise marching up and down the street wearing a kilt and that was pretty much it. The pipes hadn't been taken seriously in the folk or classical scenes. There was a bit of a contradiction because I hated seeing the pipes segregated the way they were but at the same time I was keen to keep hold of all the things we love about the pipes and the music. I wanted us all to be seen as musicians, and not have the separation between a piper, a fiddler, a drummer or singer, a guitarist or a trombone player. A musician is a musician, regardless of the instrument they play."

Finlay reckons it's important that pipers are seen in exactly the same way as all other musicians, but he does realise that there were hurdles to be overcome when the pipes started to be played more with other instruments. "There are issues that any musician needs to deal with when playing in ensemble and there is always a compromise, or at the very least there may have to be a compromise. Presently it's making sure you are in tune. That sounds like a very basic thing for a musician, and it is. We can argue the facts about equally tempered instruments versus just intonation, but what I am talking about on a practical level for a piper is getting their pipes in concert pitch in B flat."

We need to get a bit technical here, but Finlay MacDonald reckons that an understanding of what comes next is vital if the bagpipes are to be recognised as a musical instrument like any other, and if the professional piper that his degree course is producing year after year is going to be able to fit into musical ensembles not just in Scotland but all over the world. "For about four hundred years there has been a recognised system of tuning in the classical Western musical scene which is that concert pitch A vibrates at 440 Hz. If you are in Scotland playing a violin and you go to America to play with an orchestra you know you are going to be in tune. It's a standardisation. The natural home for the pipe chanter is a bit higher than concert A, in fact it's a bit higher than B flat, and I'm saying that in order to compromise and play with other instruments we have to try to get our natural pitch down a little bit and be in tune with everyone else."

Although a move down to B flat would help, many non-piping musicians think that even that pitch is too sharp and it would make more sense for the pipes to join them in A. Finlay MacDonald reckons that might be a step too far. "Getting to B flat is doable but needs work, getting to A would need a new chanter, no question."

For Finlay the debate on pitch is the first of a number of technical issues that need to be better understood by the piping world. "Pitch is completely measurable and there is no argument about that. What about tone? How do you measure or describe tone? It's aesthetic rather than measurable. It's sweet or warm or robust or rich, and that's why we need to understand what we're saying and the terms we're using. For example, at competitions the pitch has been going up all the time and I think it's because people have been saying 'I don't want to sound flat' compared to the band that has just finished. But that assumes flat is bad. What about tone? We can't replace pitch with tone. You could be playing with an instrument that has a sharper pitch but doesn't have the richness of tone, or you can have a flatter pitch that is richer."

Pipers also need to be able to tell other musicians they are playing with what key they intend to play their tunes in. "We have keys that we can play in, bunches of notes in combinations that make tunes sound different. So 'Scotland the Brave' is in A major, 'Andy Renwick's Ferret' is in A minor, it still finishes on A and A is still the tonic, but the third note on the scale is flattened and that's what determines major or minor. The first note or last note can be an indicator, and the last note probably more indicative of key. 'The Jig of Slurs' is in D, it sounds pretty upbeat and happy, so it's probably D major rather than D minor. The way we can definitely tell is to look at the third note in the scale. It's F and it's F sharp on the pipes so that's a D major. This tune actually changes key to G in the third part and you can hear that quite easily. 'Scotland the Brave' is in A major because A to C is the third and it's a C sharp, so it's in major."

Whilst this type of talk might be foreign to many pipers, Finlay reckons that they can only benefit from having more technical knowledge. He also reckons that many of them currently know more than they think they do. "A lot of pipers will know a lot of this stuff, but just not know what it's called. A pipe major putting a medley together will listen and know what works together and what doesn't without necessarily knowing the name of everything he's doing in terms of key changes. There are more and more people who understand it and know the names behind it. It's important, and if you are playing at a professional level it certainly won't do you any harm, it can only do you good."

Finlay started to study the technicalities of piping, as well as the music, when he was at school, and after a particularly unsatisfactory experience with his music teacher. "I had to do three Highers to stay on at school and my choice was either Music or Management Information Studies, so no competition. I went to see the teacher and he told me I had no chance, there was no way that I, as a piper, could learn everything that I had to learn and pass the exam in one year. I told him I wanted to give it a try and he told me I had a ninety nine percent chance of failing. That just made me all the more determined to do it. He was so negative. Would you believe that he now goes around proudly telling people that he used to teach me!"

"But there was another teacher at the school, Jean Cornwell, who is what I would call an old-style classical musician. She studied with George MacIlwham, who is ex-principal flautist with the Scottish National Orchestra, as well as a keen piper. He was a real innovator who had been including pipes in classical music as early as the fifties and sixties. Jean got to hear about the problems I was having and she told me I could go and join her class, and she had a great attitude. She said that everything he told me was rubbish and that I already knew a lot of it anyway but just didn't know what it was all called. She connected what was in my head with the theory and she helped me understand how it all worked. She was amazing and got me really excited (not in a Mrs Robinson way), about lots of different music."

Although Finlay understands the theory, and recognises its importance for pipers, he also believes that it only adds value to the music if it is used positively. "It would need to be taught in a way that was accessible and in a way that still allowed us to apply our tradition to the music. If we apply the theory to the tradition or the tradition to the theory then all well and good, but if we just go down the road of hard core theory for its own sake then we would be in danger of losing the essence of what we do. I've always been a great believer that we cannot be negative, so if I learn about modes in church music it's not as if part of my tradition will go, it all becomes enhanced, and if I start learning about improvisational jazz or classical music it doesn't make me any less of a piper, it enhances my musical skill generally."

Finlay has spent his life in piping learning how to enhance his music. "The way I have always approached my piping is to try not to attach any fixed thought process to it. I don't play Highland style or folk style or competition style; I'll play how I feel. That's why I never competed. I tried it a couple of times when I was younger but I just didn't enjoy it. I felt it concentrated so much on the technique and I couldn't play the way I wanted to play because I was so worried about missing things. I think it's worth mentioning at this time as well that the word 'technique' is misused in that people assume it is about missing gracenotes. For me it's more than that, it is about how you play it as much as whether you play it. How heavy you play a strike for example, with more or less low A for emphasis. When you have that it can elevate your playing to a different level."

For Finlay it's not just about how pipers play, but about how listeners listen. "The competition system means that we always listen critically rather than for enjoyment. For a long time, and for a lot of pipers, by far the biggest outlet they have is competition, either in bands or solo competition. Many of these pipers are obsessed and conditioned by technique. We have to get into the deeper thoughts on technique, rather than looking at, and focusing on, missed gracenotes or other ornamentation."

"It seems to me that there is a lack of emotional connection from both the piper and the listener. The piper is thinking, 'I hope I don't make any mistakes. I need my playing to be really clean and tidy'. The listener is listening for mistakes and to check out technique. So someone will learn the tune exactly as it is in the Scots Guards Book and then it gets locked in their brain and they say 'that's the tune and that's how I have to play it', like it is some sort of fixed entity. There are people who take their metronomes out and make sure that they play it at the same tempo every time. I totally understand the technical perfection they are trying to achieve but what they are losing out on is the emotion, the aesthetic side and the feelings, because there is so much focus on the technique."

For Finlay there is nothing wrong with taking a tune and removing all of the gracings if you think it sounds better, but only if you understand what you're doing. "If you have the knowledge and the experience, and you can make these decisions, then it is up to you to decide how you are going to interpret the music. But I think one hundred percent that the technique needs to be taught and understood initially. I'm not against the technique; I'm just against the notion that it is fixed and not open to interpretation. What if you feel a bit fired up one day. You might want to take the tempo up a bit. But then you think — oh no, can't do that, I play that one at sixty two beats per minute. I find I struggle to listen to that type of piping because my natural inclination is to interpret the emotional side of music rather than the technical."

Part of the remit of the course that Finlay teaches is to take the tradition, teach it, and help it to move forward. To do that you have to take risks. "There should be no limits, and if I said there were it would be totally contradictory. I've heard some really crazy stuff that has made me question if it's music or not but who am I to judge, other than from personal taste. I mean one man's Red Hot Chilli Pipers is another man's Stravinsky. There is almost a bit of reverse snobbery now in the piping world and I have heard people from outside the competition world slagging it to death and saying that all these competition pipers are just robots who play mechanically."

"It's almost like they have become the snobs now and they are judging the competition guys more than they may have been judging us. Most of the competition guys I talk to, and maybe they are just saying this to me to keep me quiet, but they'll say that they don't do what I do but they appreciate it. That's all I'm asking. They don't have to like what I'm doing, just appreciate that I have the right to do it. For example, I'm not a great fan of pìobaireachd because I've never connected with it but I do understand and respect the level of knowledge and concentration that is required to deliver a great pìobaireachd. I hear the likes of Roddy MacLeod and Angus MacColl do it all the time and it impresses the hell out of me, but I don't play it."

Although Finlay doesn't connect personally with pìobaireachd he hopes that he has managed to strike the correct balance between the emotional and the technical in the degree course that he teaches at the Royal Conservatoire of Scotland in Glasgow. "Teaching pipes as part of the degree course has helped pipers understand the theory, as well as put it into practice. I think that the way it is being taught is close enough to the folk music ideals and beliefs and it also takes ideas from the Western music theory to help pipers make informed decisions on what you are doing as a musician. The course has done that. I think it is very easy to criticise from the outside and say that it is diluting our tradition but I think that we are living it now. We are living in a very exciting time for music in Scotland. I don't think we should use the fear of losing something to stop us creating what I think of as the new tradition or the continuing tradition. For the tradition to go forward it has to change and if I don't do it someone else will be doing it."

As far as Finlay is concerned there are lots of musicians out there doing just that at the moment, helping to push the tradition forward, particularly as far as new music is concerned. "If you think forward a hundred and fifty years when we're all dead and look back at this time then I think that they will think that it's incredible the amount of good stuff coming out. There's me and my pal Chris Stout and there's Chris Armstrong, Ross Ainslie and Ally Hutton, and Kyle Warren. Then the other guys like Neil Dickie, Murray Blair, Michael Grey, Mark Saul, James McKenzie and Calum MacCrimmon. Why all these names? Well they just write good tunes. I think it's as simple as that."

"Then you have the big guns; Gordon Duncan, Fred Morrison and Roddy MacDonald. I think that these last three guys are different. With all three of them, their tunes are not that far removed from the tradition, they are still recognised as jigs or reels or whatever, we're not talking about avant-garde experimentation, although there is a lot of that out there as well. Some of it is great. Matthew Welsh is pushing the boat a bit, as is Fraser Fifield, but what Fred, Gordon and Roddy have, or had, is almost comfortable. It's new but we feel safe with it. Gordon was pushing boundaries, but in musical exploration terms it's still a jig or a reel. Okay it messed a bit with the chromatics, rhythmic patterns and modal shapes so it seems a bit more out there, but they're not really outrageous, they're just great tunes."

The great thing about the degree course in Finlay's mind is that it is producing graduates who are all-round musicians rather than just pipers, and musicians who are able to go and take their place in the world of work when they graduate. "For serious musicians looking to make a career in music there are business issues that need to be explored, and we like to think that the course gives the students experience in how this all works. For example, you could be doing a gig at Celtic Connections and there is a guaranteed audience there, it's like a funded project with a guaranteed income and no risk. But for two years now Chris Stout and I have done a gig in Carradale. It's a lovely wee hall that holds just over two hundred people. We can't tell them that our fee is £X and that it's set in stone and they need to cover it, because it's just not going to happen. You know these people are promoting for the benefit of their community. So we sit down and look at what is going to realistically work for all of us. How many tickets can you sell? What's the price, who is doing the bar, and will we do a split on the door or a guaranteed fee? You have to look at every gig individually and ask what price we can do it for that will cover our costs, make us some money. The musicians have to understand how it all works and how they can do it without putting the local promoters out as well. I think the students are quite switched on to all of this but it's a different scene from when I left because there were less people doing it then. The year I left and got my first album out there were only ten of us on the course, now there are between fifty and sixty in total and we're sitting, usually, with between ten and twenty pipers."

That means that there are more and more musicians looking to pick up a fairly static number of gigs. "Are we producing too many? I don't know if I'd say that but we need to realise that there are lots of different paths people can take with this degree and it's not just about a guaranteed job at the end. I had a pal at school who kept saying that he would do four years at law school, then a diploma, and then he's sorted for life. For us it's completely different. I'm very clear at telling it like it really is at auditions, or at open days if parents come up. 'You have to be very clear about this; you will probably end up doing lots of different things here. You won't go to college then come out as a musician and start to play in a band for the rest of your life. You might, but what is more likely is that you will do a bit of teaching, you'll do some gigs and you'll do some recording. You might get involved in some community projects and you might get involved in broadcasting or research or arts management.' The portfolio career they call it, where there is not one income stream. I guess pipers are luckier in a way because there are more local authorities introducing pipes to the school system and guys like Chris Gibb, Gordon Bruce and Cammy Drummond are getting jobs now."

With the Scottish Music Degree producing some of the best players we have seen in recent years, Finlay MacDonald is really positive about the piping scene in general. "Piping is more popular than it has ever been, the standard is higher than it has ever been, and there is much more variety in accepted styles. The whole piping world has become much more accepting. It's more forward looking while still maintaining and excelling in the traditional side of things."

There are a few people at the forefront of this popularity. "Fred Morrison stands out for me. He has such a unique style and take on things, he has the whole package. He plays with great tone and emotion, and that's what really gets it for me. I think he's a great performer. He displays this haphazard attitude but he's really organised and when he's on song there's nobody to touch him. Willie Morrison, Ian Morrison, Roddy MacLeod, Willie McCallum, Angus MacColl and Gordon Walker all play at a really high standard and the sound they have is so advanced."

As well as a very busy time running the degree course at the Royal Conservatoire of Scotland, Finlay is still pursuing lots of creative projects, although in a different way. "The days of getting a phone call asking if I can go to Algeria in two days' time are pretty much over. I guess I do miss that in a way, or at least I can remember it fondly, because what I have now is a situation where I'm lucky that I have a full-time job that covers the bills. Also, I'm married with a family now and my focus has changed, and the way that I'm doing it has changed. I'm doing fewer gigs than I was ten years ago but they are gigs I would rather be doing. I think I'm playing much better now than I ever have been."

And he's now doing it without the Finlay Macdonald Band. "I had reached the limit of where I could take my band. The actual playing on stage wasn't a problem but the day-to-day management was becoming an issue. I think that it is important to keep control because if you give that up to an agent or manager and they haven't dealt with the promoter the way you would have done then you are instantly tarred with a brush that you might not want to be tarred with. I thought I had reached the end of my creative input with that and I made a conscious decision that instead of flogging it and keeping it going I would stop. That has allowed me to spend a lot more time concentrating on my own playing and analysing what I was doing, and I hadn't done that for a while. I didn't do many high profile gigs for a year or so and didn't know where it was going to lead. It was a hard thing to do because I could easily have had a couple of gigs a month but it was emotionally straining. It had been nothing to do with the music or the people, it was just that I was looking for something else from my own playing."

As well as reckoning that he is close to finding what he was looking for with his own music, Finlay also has a treasure chest of stories that could fill a whole other book. "I remember doing a gig at The Arches about six years ago at Piping Live! with At First Light, John McSherry's band. It was one of these great nights. We all seemed to be playing really well and in the zone that I've heard sportsmen talk about. I felt there was no barrier between my head and my fingers. The pipes were great, there was some great improvisation going on, and it just seemed really slick. It passed really slowly and it all felt so right. I've no idea what it sounded like to everyone else but for me it was great."

It's not always the quality of the music that makes the gig memorable. "There was an episode at Tartan Week in New York a couple of years ago. I'd been asked to go along to Grand Central Station to pipe someone on to the stage at this event that was on. The oldest bottle of whisky in the world was up for auction, or something like that. I was backstage getting ready to play and there were lots of people about, and this guy with funny hair was in front of me. I thought I recognised him from the piping scene and proceeded to ask him what he did. He told me he did a bit of this and a bit of that that and we chewed the fat for a minute, and

I told him how rough I was feeling after a heavy night with Simon McKerrell. Then the stage manager came along and told me we were ready to go and I heard an announcement welcoming Donald Trump to the stage. That's where I had recognised the hair! Then last year in the same week I played in Glasgow with Bryan Adams and P Diddy. Musically they were not great gigs, but as events they were fantastic to do — I think the P Diddy one was transmitted to twenty-seven million viewers. Regardless of the gig I still get a kick out of it. I don't know if you call it nerves or if it's anticipation. You want to enjoy it and you want the audience to enjoy it. You care about every note you play and you want to make sure it's as good as it can be."

Iain MacFadyen

Iain MacFadyen reckons he is a very lucky man. Since he left the army in 1959 he only ever had two jobs — one with Glasgow City Council Transport Department and the other teaching bagpipes in Kyle of Lochalsh — and both of his employers gave him regular time off when he needed it to go and play. "My life would be completely different if I hadn't applied for this school job in 1972. I don't know where I would have been. It was a great move to come up to this neck of the woods but I hadn't really given any thought to making it my living. I had started teaching in the College of Piping when Seumas McNeill was Principal, and I applied for a job in the schools when they were just introducing piping. It was really my brother John and Seumas McNeill who were at the forefront of that drive to have piping in schools. I applied for the job up here and got it."

By the time he arrived in Kyle, Iain was already well established as one of the country's top players, with a fantastic track record in the major competitions. "I won my first Gold Medal the first time I played for it in Inverness in 1957. I was very lucky because you can play for it for years and get nothing and I won it first time out. Then my brother John won it in 1962 or 1963. Duncan, my other brother, won it in 1966. It's the first time, and in fact the only time, that three brothers have won a Gold Medal."

Not only was Iain established as one of the best, but he hailed from a family that produced several of the best in recent generations. "I'm one of a family of ten, five boys and five girls. John was the oldest, then Hector, Duncan, Archie, then me. One of my sisters, Freena, also played. My father was a piper but he wasn't a great player. He had no one to teach him. He went to sea as a young man and they didn't have the teaching capabilities in those days. I went to private lessons and my first teacher was the blind piper Archie McNeill, Seumas's uncle. Well, my father started me then I went to Archie. I was late in starting by today's standards. Kids today begin in primary four or five, maybe seven or eight years old, but I was twelve or thirteen. I was a fast learner because by the time I was sixteen I had picked up all of the amateur prizes, and I turned professional when I was sixteen. I got a prize at Oban in the Gold Medal when I was seventeen so I must have been a fast learner!"

Iain MacFadyen

Iain was taught by Archie McNeill for the first couple of years he was learning but then moved on to a succession of other teachers, each of whom was able to add something else to the young man's musical skills. However, it all started with Archie. "I would play and he would sit beside me, then he would come and stand in front of me and put his hands over my hands so that he could feel how far I was lifting them off the chanter. He had a wonderful ear and he could tell if I was making a crossing sound. I think his other senses were obviously sharper because he couldn't see. I went to him for about two years and he was a great teacher. He gave me my first pìobaireachd, 'The Lament For The Old Sword', and then, after about two years, my dad was in the pipers club in Glasgow on a Saturday night and Archie MacNeill was there. He said to my father that he thought it was time I went elsewhere and he suggested I went to Peter Bain from Skye. I went to Peter for maybe two or three years. He was a great teacher of light music, he wasn't really into pìobaireachd and I was quite keen to learn both, so I went to Roddy MacDonald from Glasgow Police for lessons. I never really had one teacher, I went to Duncan Johnstone for hornpipes and jigs, and I think all that was good for me because when it came to competition I was versatile and could play pretty well across all disciplines."

No one would question that statement, and the fact that he has probably won more prizes across the disciplines than any other player would back up Iain's view that he was a great all-rounder. What is fascinating is that he has achieved this success without ever having a disciplined practice regime. "I wasn't a great one for practice. I certainly wouldn't play for hours on end, but I would learn the tunes and then practice them for an hour and a half each day, or at least half an hour even if I was going out. I just picked them up and played what I fancied, and I very rarely practiced my light music, mostly pìobaireachd. I might not play the whole tune or even play it in order. One night I might play the crunluath and the next night I'd play the ground then the next night I'd play a variation. I remember getting 'The Lament for the Harp Tree' one year in the Silver Chanter, and that's one of the longest tunes. I never played it right through from start to finish when I was practicing, and I won. I used to play variations, stop for a fag, and start again, but never the whole thing until the day of the competition. It was just too long to play in the house."

After serving his apprenticeship as a joiner with Harland and Wolff in Glasgow, Iain, in common with everyone else his age at that time, had to go and do his two years National Service. Even then the luck he referred to earlier helped him out. "I got my calling up papers to go to the Royal Scots in Edinburgh and I had to go there in the October, the 19th. In the September of that year I went to The Northern Meetings and won the Gold Medal with Lieutenant Colonel David Murray as one of the adjudicators. When the results came out he came over to me and asked when I was due for National Service. I told him I had my papers for the Royal Scots, and he asked me how I fancied the Cameron Highlanders. Well I had two years to do and it didn't really matter where I went, so he said, 'Leave it with me'. A couple of weeks later I got a letter from the War Office telling me to report to Cameron Barracks in Inverness, and not Dreghorn Barracks in Edinburgh."

That was a move that certainly did Iain's playing no harm. "It was great because we had a good pipe band. John McDougall and Willie MacDonald were with me and we did a lot of piping in the Army. I would have been able to play in Edinburgh if I had gone to the Royal Scots, but the band wasn't as good. As far as David Murray was concerned I was a piper first and a soldier second. If I'd gone to the Royal Scots I think it would have been the other way round. He let us go round the games to compete. John and I won a lot so it was great publicity for the Regiment."

As well as his solo playing, Iain kept up with the pipe band world when he left the Army, playing with both Red Hackle and Glasgow Corporation Transport Pipe Band, latterly as pipe major, until he moved up to Kyle of Lochalsh in 1973. He reckons that the pipe band competition scene has changed immensely since he was involved, and the changes are not all positive. "It was nothing like it is today; there were no medleys in those days, only the MSR. You submitted three marches, three strathspeys and three reels. Pipe band playing today is completely different, you have to be totally committed. I think some bands do go over the score. I listened to the bands at Glasgow Green this year and I just thought that with what they were playing it was getting away from piping altogether. They were changing parts of tunes and changing tempo and maybe having three or four time signatures in one tune, it kind of bastardises it as far I am concerned. I have a very traditional approach. I'm not averse to what they're doing, but you have to be very careful, with the way that a lot of the young ones are coming out with all this folky playing."

For Iain, this also highlights the difference between solo piping and pipe band playing. "You don't have to be a good solo player to be a good band player because in a lot of cases, in a pipe band, as long as the notes are all correct you will get away with missing out a doubling. You won't get away with that in solo playing. If there are five pipers playing I wouldn't be able to tell if you missed a doubling but you would hear it in the solos.

Iain is also concerned about the lack of prominence pìobaireachd has in today's teaching schedules. "They're not teaching pìobaireachd as much as they should be, nothing like it. I'm not sure whether anyone will be left playing pìobaireachd fifty years from now. If you take a lot of the top bands, they are very good bands, but I doubt if there are two people in that band that could play a couple of pìobaireachds. I mean the likes of Simon Fraser University Pipe Band, they have a lot of good pìobaireachd players, and so do Field Marshal Montgomery, but there are a lot of good bands coming up where there will be very few pìobaireachd players."

That would be sad for piping. "There is a magazine out called the International Piper. I found some old copies, and I saw a piece on a recital I did in London. It said that I had given a good recital and my pipes were great and that I had played three pìobaireachds. You would never play three at a recital today but that was the kind of thing we used to do. Maybe I couldn't play twenty or thirty hornpipes or jigs the way these young guys can today. It doesn't matter who they are but they'll play one short pìobaireachd at most, usually because folk don't generally want to sit and listen to three in a recital these days. That's why I think there has been a change in our attitude to pìobaireachd playing."

Although Iain has spent the best part of his adult life teaching bagpipes, he is still sure that the teaching system itself might have something to do with the decline in the quality of pìobaireachd playing. "You have to look at who are being appointed as instructors in the schools because a lot of them are not great pìobaireachd players, and if they are not that keen on it themselves then they are hardly going to spend a lot of time teaching it in the schools. Not all of the instructors are of the same quality. I think most of them come through the Academy. It used to be the case that you would get a teaching job based on your results in competition and that doesn't happen now. If you take a successful competitor and someone out the Academy going for the same job, then the person with the degree will get it. I don't know if that's always a good thing. I don't know enough about who is on the panel or who is making the appointments but I think that's what's happening. The fact that I am not a qualified teacher has not made any difference to my ability to teach others. I think that nowadays when they make appointments they seem to be hell-bent on taking on people from the Academy who have a degree and there seems to be an awful lot of them who are not as good as some without degrees."

Having said that, Iain does recognise the fact that there

are some excellent young players coming through the ranks now. Partly because they are naturally skilled players, but partly because the quality of the instrument is such an important factor. "I think the quality has improved and there are a lot of fine young players now, like Finlay Johnston or Callum Beaumont. These guys play in a band as well; they're not just solo players. I don't think Finlay will be any better than I was at his age, but he will have a better instrument than I would have had. I think that's what won Donald MacPherson so many prizes, his instrument. I know lots of players who were as good as Donald MacPherson but they didn't win the prizes that Donald won because they didn't have the instrument. Roddy MacLeod is the same in that he has won a lot of prizes because of the quality of his instrument, although he is a top class player. The reeds are better, the chanter pitch has changed, the drones haven't changed that much because most of the top players are playing old pipes, but the moisture control systems have been introduced and that has made a difference, and the plastic reeds have helped. The reeds don't get wet in the same way — you will very seldom hear a top class player today with a bass drone that stops, but in my day it happened all the time. That was you finished if your drone stopped, any drone. You have to start and finish with three drones."

Since we're using luck as a recurring theme through Iain's story, (although as Arnold Palmer once famously said 'the more I practice the luckier I seem to get', so maybe Iain is being unfair on himself), it is useful to relate the tale of the pipes that took him to so many prizes. "I have always been lucky with my pipes in that I have never had to spend huge amounts of time getting them going. I had an old set of MacDougall's and then I had the first set that Bob Hardie made in 1947. When he started in business with John Weatherston he made a set, and I've got them to this day. They were nickel and silver. He sent them through to an exhibition in Edinburgh. They then came back to Glasgow and my father bought them for me in 1947. They cost fifty pounds, and that is the instrument that I won two Gold Medals and a couple of Glenfiddich Championships with. Fifty pounds was a lot of money in 1947 because my father would probably have been earning around five pounds a week."

Even the other set of pipes that Iain uses came to him by no small amount of good fortune. "My uncle Allan, who was a clerk of works with Argyll Council, was in Mull one day and this old woman said her house was getting cleared out and they were having a bit of a fire out in the garden. Alan looked out and saw the bonfire and at the tip there were three drones. No bag, no chanter, just three drones. He asked what they were and she said 'Just an old set of pipes my husband had lying around'. He said he wanted to give her something for them, and she said 'Just give me ten pounds'. No bag or stocks, just the drones. I got them from Uncle Allan in 1940 and they were MacDougall drones. I still have them here. I have won a lot of prizes with these pipes. I'm still playing them and they are absolutely beautiful, plain ivory. I played them mostly in my competing days."

Iain stopped competing in 1987, thirty years after he won his first Gold Medal, but he still plays regularly, and reckons that his playing is still good enough to win a chanter competition, however he's not sure how it would stand up to scrutiny on the pipes. That first victory in the Gold Medal in 1957 is still a highlight, even after more than half a century. "Winning the Gold Medal in Inverness the first time stands out because I wasn't even going to go; it was my brother John who coaxed me into it. I had been playing in Glasgow and my father said, 'Just go and keep your brother company' and I never in my wildest dreams thought I would win the Medal. I played the 'End of the Great Bridge'. I never even gave winning a thought when I finished playing, I was just happy to get through my performance from what I can remember; after all it was over fifty years ago. I tell you, I was more excited just going to Inverness with John; it was a long drive from Glasgow. I think it took about eight hours."

He is also the proud owner of one of only three special National Mod Banners. "I got great satisfaction winning the Mod Banner. It was 1968 and that was the first year they ever had it. It was just a march, strathspey and reel you had to play and it was held at Aviemore. It was sponsored by John Player, the cigarette company. They sponsored it for three years and I think only three of us have these banners. I got the first one, and John Burgess and Iain MacLeod have the other two, and then John Players withdrew their support."

Having won more competitions than most players before or since, Iain has sympathy for a few great players who never managed to come good on Gold Medal days. "It is very difficult to win a Medal. I think Donald MacPherson played twenty times before he won it and yet he won seven or eight Clasps. He just found it really difficult to get a Medal. John Garroway was one of the best players I ever knew who never won a Medal. He played with Glasgow Police, and was a great player, but I think he was second six times or something like that. Jimmy Young was another very good player who was second three times; twice when I won my medal, and also when Duncan won, so three times he came second to a MacFadyen."

A Piper's Tale

Iain is an avid visitor to piping competitions all over the country these days, although how he deals with the day depends on whether he is a spectator or a judge. "I don't think I would sit still and listen to all ten pìobaireachds at The Glenfiddich if I'm not judging. It's a long day. This year I judged the pìobaireachd and did sit through the whole MSR competition in the afternoon. It was amazing, the difference sitting at the back of the hall. Out of the five prize-winners I had picked three, but I had two on my list that got nothing."

While Iain still enjoys judging these major events, he is in no doubt that it can make for a long and stressful day. "It's not an easy job. For a start you need total concentration to make sure that the player has not missed anything out, and that can be a danger when you know a tune well because you could switch off, especially when it is a tune where there are bars repeated or lines repeated. You might think 'Did he repeat that there? I can't remember.' and that is the only problem with having one judge. I would happily judge on my own as long as I had a reader with me to confirm that the competitor had not made a mistake, but on your own it is a very difficult thing to do. The major competitions all have three judges but I judged the Silver Chanter on my own three years ago. I had a reader with me and that helped."

"We don't often argue, but that's why we have three judges, just in case we do. I don't think I have ever judged a major competition where each judge has had a different result. I've judged where one judge is different from the other two, but the one who differs will have the other competitor in the top three. What I will sometimes do is ask my co-adjudicators to pick five names each and I'll do the same. Then we'll see if at least we have the same five. We then start to place them, and it's amazing that you will usually be pretty near it. If we're all different then we need to start to discuss why and come to an agreement. I would say that in all my years judging I have never fallen out with anyone or had any real disputes over results. I've never left a bench thinking 'that wasn't my result', I've always left happy."

Iain is in no doubt as to what he is looking for when sitting on the bench these days. "You need to have the musicality because it is musical competition. You have to be technically sound as well and you can't expect to win a major competition if you miss out three or four technical movements. Likewise you can't expect to win a major competition if your performance is technically correct but has no music in it. It depends on the level, but I can't imagine someone at the top level playing a whole tune with no music. Everyone knows when you've missed something out but they

100

don't always know when it's not musical because that's subjective, so if I had to choose between a technically flawed performance with music or a technically perfect performance with no music, I think I would have to go with the music."

Although Iain still enjoys judging, and his position as one of the senior judges in the circuit, it's not something that will continue indefinitely. "There will come a time when I stop judging, when I can't hear them play or can't read the book. It's a funny thing because I always remember when I was competing and I would see judges coming up to the platform. I remember looking at DR McLennan or Bobby Reid thinking 'Why are these old guys judging'. They were maybe seventy. I'm far more than that and I'm still one of the senior judges. I think there is a better standard of player judging now because in my day a lot of people were judging not on their ability of piping but because of who they were. There was a lot of doffing the cap and if you were a lawyer or whatever then you could judge the local piping, but that won't happen now. There is far more respect for judges. Young people will come to a bench now and see the likes of John Wilson or Hugh McCallum sitting there and they will be quite happy to be able to play like them and to have them judging as well. When I was competing there were times I would turn up and not recognise any of the judges."

Although Iain reckons there is a better standard of player judging these days, he's not as convinced about the playing standard at the top. "I don't think that the playing is as good as it was when I was growing up, but I think that the instrument is much better and that makes the playing sound better. I think the standard of playing in the seventies and eighties was better than it is today, especially in pìobaireachd playing. Think of all the players. John MacLellan, Donald MacLeod, Jimmy Macgregor, Iain MacLeod, my two brothers, Hugh McCallum, Bob Brown, you don't have that calibre of player today. Your Angus MacColl, Willie McCallum and Stuart Liddell and the like would compare but there are not nearly as many. All these guys were top class players but today at The Glenfiddich you could pick your winners from five or six of the guys there. Having said that, there are more good young players. When I was playing as an amateur you might have got ten players in a competition whereas now there might be thirty and lots of them are really good."

Iain still enjoys putting in the groundwork that produces these really good players. "I've taught literally hundreds. Darrach Urquhart, my son Ian, Anne McKay, John Fisher, whose father was a doctor in Dunvegan, young Niall Stewart, and Decker Forrest, all mainly for pìobaireachd. I like to maintain my values when I teach. That's important to me and it's important to them. I teach them a competition style of playing. I'm not against pipe bands, I think they are great for the kids and it teaches them independence. It makes them look after themselves and their pipes and it helps them to learn a lot of tunes, but I tell them that I am going to teach them as if they are going to be a competing piper."

Colin MacLellan

If anyone in this book was going to feel parental pressure to pick up a chanter you would have thought it would have been Colin MacLellan, whose father, Captain John MacLellan, spent years in charge of piping in the British Army at Edinburgh Castle. This is not the case. "I started playing at George Heriot's School in Edinburgh because it was offered long before the days when schools had full-time instructors. The gentleman who taught me was Jack Crichton, John D Crichton to give him his full name, who was quite an influential figure in the Royal Scottish Pipe Band Association because he founded the Knightswood Juvenile Band."

Jack Crichton was a technical teacher at George Heriot's, what we would have called woodwork back then, and he had a novel method of deciding which of the boys who wanted to join his class were suitable. When Jack came into Colin's class and asked who wanted to learn to play, around half of the class put their hands up. But Jack couldn't teach as many as that. "Because he was the woodwork teacher he had all of these little sticks with holes bored in them where the holes in the chanter would be and he showed us all how to play the scale. We would come back in a week and he would choose the boys who he wanted to take lessons."

Colin hadn't realised that there would be a selection process. "I did get a bit scared that I wouldn't get chosen because I thought it would be a bit embarrassing for my dad so I went away and practiced like hell on this bit of stick. I don't think my father was all that impressed with Jack's little stick trick."

Looking back on the episode it was only later that Colin realised that Jack and his father were actually very close friends, and so the chances of him not being picked for lessons were probably quite slim. Jack taught Colin until he was fifteen or sixteen and had started to compete regularly in the under-fifteen and under-eighteen competitions. By his own admission, he wasn't the most committed of players in those days. "I was like most kids that started. There was a point where I would always do enough to get by and it was only when I started to compete in the amateur competitions that I got keen about it. I had played in some chanter competitions and they had been okay, but when I played in the

---

'fifteen and under' and 'eighteen and under' sort of stuff the first couple didn't really go very well. That gave me a kick and made me knuckle down because I knew that I should have been doing better. I got very keen about it all."

It was only at this stage that his dad became involved with Colin's piping. "I think there must have been pressure to do well because of my father, but my parents didn't put pressure on me to either play or to become a good player. My dad didn't get involved in my teaching at all until the point when I started to play in amateur competitions and then he took a bit of interest. That had been a good thing because it doesn't always work when parents get involved. He had been happy with the way things had been going up until then."

It was round about then that Colin began practicing with other fine players with whom he maintains close links to this day, as well as some who have slipped from the scene. "At school there were three or four super players who were every bit as good as I was, guys you have never heard off who left after school - Roy Anderson and Jim Williamson were two of them. They did really well in all the inter-school competitions. Then Euan Anderson came along and later Iain and Gregor Speirs. Jack taught us all on a Friday afternoon for an hour and a half, not as part of the school curriculum, it was an extra activity."

It was as part of these Friday afternoon sessions that Colin got his first taste of teaching. "We played in the school band and as we got older Jack let us take on some of the teaching activities ourselves. When I was fourteen or fifteen he was handing some of the pupils on to me and that's how I got into teaching piping. It was really valuable being exposed to teaching at that sort of age, and being responsible for the product. Having been involved a bit since, in teaching at private schools, I look back at that whole period and think that Heriot's School and Jack Crichton produced some great stuff on those Friday afternoons."

The other thing that Colin remembers about these Friday afternoon lessons, and that has changed dramatically for thousands of youngsters all over the world today, is that they were free. "It's an interesting point about the way money changes hands today. In those days people weren't making a living from piping. They were doing it because they wanted to, but I don't think there is anything wrong with charging, and I think you have to if it is the way you make a living."

Colin recognises that there has to be a place for people who do it for pleasure, and in Scotland, as in a lot of other places round the world, there are lots of bands working night after night teaching a new generation of players, and it doesn't happen by magic. "There are a lot of people doing sterling work with these bands, far more than are teaching professionally, and they are all doing it for free."

The introduction of professional teachers, which was happening slowly while Colin was at school, has helped to change the image of piping, and pipers, in the wider community. "I remember that when I went to school it wasn't a particularly cool thing to be doing. You kept it a bit of a secret because you were seen to be a bit of a geek, even in a school in Scotland's capital city, but now it's seen as a status symbol and nobody would make fun of anybody playing the pipes. I remember when I was teaching in three high schools in Glengarry County in Ontario and it was the first time I saw that it had status. I remember thinking back to my time at school and thinking things had really changed for the better."

Colin MacLellan had no great life plan to get into teaching piping, despite enjoying his early experience. He was invited to teach at the Thousand Islands School for the Performing Arts in Canada in the summer of 1977 and he ended up staying for twenty-two years. It also gave him his introduction to pipe band playing, which had been denied to him in Scotland, partly due to the only disagreement he had with his father over his piping. "At the time I had only ever played in the school band at Heriot's but I had got friendly with a couple of Canadian guys, Scott MacAulay and John Elliott, who were playing with Muirhead and Sons."

"I wanted to join Muirhead's but my father wasn't interested in me playing in a pipe band at all. It was the age when it was seen that if you played in a pipe band it would be to the detriment of your solo career, which has since proved not to be the case, but in those days there hadn't been a lot of people who were successful in a solo career and who also played in a pipe band. The Muirhead's guys were some of the first people to expose the lie that you couldn't be a good solo player and play in a band. One of the reasons I wanted to join them was because guys like Donald McBride, Robert Wallace and these Canadian guys were playing and they were getting a lot of stuff from Bob Hardie."

When Colin arrived in Canada, Bill Livingstone had just taken over as pipe major of the City of Toronto Pipe Band, and he was really intrigued with the work that Bill was doing with the structure of medleys, especially the way they were involving pìobaireachds like the 'Desperate Battle' and 'MacIntosh's Lament'. He joined the band. "It was a four hour drive from where I lived in Ontario to Toronto but I went to town as often as I could and I played with them for a while. They were the precursor to the General Motors band that eventual became the 78th Fraser Highlanders. That was my start in pipe bands and it didn't affect my solo playing at all, in fact it probably affected it positively because some of the music we played was difficult stuff and it wasn't our choice to play it. You didn't have the luxury of saying 'This tune suits me so I'll learn it but this one doesn't, so I won't'. We had to learn all of the tunes that the band had chosen to play. It was a very good band with a lot of good players so I do think it was a positive thing."

When the City of Toronto Band had a few problems, before its transition to 78th Fraser Highlanders, Colin stopped playing with them and started teaching in schools in Glengarry County, much closer to home. He took the band to the top of Grade 2 in Canada and remembers his time there fondly. "At the time I was twenty-five and the kids in the band were about fifteen. Now I'm fifty-five and they are all forty-five or so and they have become some of my best friends. There are only ten years between us and the gap in ages seems a lot smaller now than it did then."

Colin MacLellan continued his work with younger players when he came back to Scotland after two decades. He and his wife Jenny had already made the decision to make the move when he took a call from Roddy MacLeod at the National Piping Centre. "Roddy explained that they were in the process of setting up the degree course in conjunction with what was then the Royal Scottish Academy of Music and Drama. They were looking for some help and wanted to know if I was interested in getting involved. They were at the stage where they had decided it was going to happen, and it was planned, but none of the structure had been put in place. I'd studied for degrees in Political Science and Education in Canada which was why Roddy MacLeod was keen to get me involved. I was there for eighteen months or so, liaising with Roddy and RSAMD, organising the first classes and putting the structures in place so that the National Piping Centre could undergo the verification process and could become affiliated with an institute of higher learning."

They had pretty much started with a blank sheet of paper which was great for all concerned since the National Piping Centre was still in its infancy and still trying to find its way. "Roddy was really good at structuring meetings during the week." Colin remembers. "One of the things we were doing at the time was writing the tutor book, which actually had nothing to do with the degree programme. It did allow an hour or two a week when the whole business of the Centre would get dropped and people would meet and discuss ideas for the book. That way you got eight or nine people's ideas on how to teach piping all put into that tutor, and everyone had input into the degree course as well."

Colin MacLellan

Round about that time, the National Piping Centre held what they reckon was the world's first distance lesson on computer. Colin remembers it being a very complicated process involving in the region of thirty-two phone lines at one time, which was the cost of thirty-two international calls. "The cost of the lesson was about £140 for half an hour, a far cry from the Skype lessons that take place all over the world today with extreme ease and at a fraction of that cost."

If the introduction of teaching in the schools in the seventies helped to change piping's image, it was nothing compared to the changes when it was introduced as a degree course, according to Colin MacLellan. "It's a great thing. When the students come out of that programme they are all-rounders. They know about the history, they know about writing music, and they all play other instruments as well as the pipes. They know a lot about Gaelic and history but most importantly it's a performance degree, so on top of all the learning theory they also have to learn to perform."

The standard is unbelievably high according to Colin. "Every time I have gone there as an examiner, I have been stunned at the level of performance. From the recitals in first year, where they play for fifteen or twenty minutes, right up to final year where they play for an hour, the standard is incredible. The improvement in standard when people have immersed themselves in the course for a time, and spent time playing and practicing, is also great to see. It's not just performance that's important, because they are also getting involved in the whole culture of the music. It is the equal of what you will hear anywhere."

This high standard, and the increased competition for places, is introducing a whole new generation of potential top performers. "There are some really good people coming up. Ally Henderson from the degree course, Finlay Johnston and Callum Beaumont. I'm really pleased for him because he was twelve when he came and played with Lothian and Borders Police. Cameron Drummond is a fantastic player as well. There are all sorts of them; there is no shortage."

It's not just their technique that impresses him. "It's the musicality that sets these people apart. Everyone has perfect finger technique. It's got to the stage where if you don't have perfect technique and a more or less perfect bagpipe then you are kind of wasting your time. So it's music that sets people apart. In a way I'm hesitant to say you can't teach it, but you have to have it inherently, and that's what's setting apart the young people at the top."

MacLellan believes that this concentration on the music is filtering through to competition, and impacting the way that competitions are being judged today. "I think very few competitions are decided on the bagpipe or the technique; I think the vast majority are decided on music."

Mention of Callum Beaumont, who played with Lothian and Borders Police Pipe Band under Colin's leadership, naturally led to a discussion of the now defunct operation, once one of the proudest bands in the country. "When I came back to Scotland I was asked to be pipe major of Lothian and Borders Pipe Band, which was in crisis. It had been demoted to Grade 2 and I'm not sure if poisoned chalice is the right phrase but it seemed to have been difficult for every pipe major since 1975 with that band. It was something that I was asked to do, and I was keen to do because of the history of the band and its position in Edinburgh."

Colin had no real connection with the band when he was learning his trade as a piper and growing up in Edinburgh, he was slightly too young to become involved in a police band at that time and they weren't really looking for new players. Even if they had been it would have been serving officers that attracted their attention rather than civilians. "I took over from Kenny McBride and the job was to get the band back into Grade 1. I had the support of a lot of friends who came to the band — my wife Jenny, Euan Anderson, Innes Smith, Iain Speirs, Gregor Speirs, the two young Beaumont lads. They all came along, and so we were able to win enough quickly enough to get promoted back to Grade 1. I was there for five years and by 2005 I handed it over to Keith Dawes. Since then it has had a succession of pipe majors. One of the things that needs to be said is that it's a myth that it has been in long and gradual decline. If you listen to the recordings you'll find that the band, and each subsequent band, has, in general, been better than the one before. When the band played with Spirit of Scotland Pipe Band at Celtic Connections in 2012 the performance was top notch, the best performance the band has ever put on."

The debate about whether the band's demise was due in the end to the move to the single Police Force in Scotland or not will rumble on for years but Colin MacLellan's view is not in doubt. "I think the reality is that if we weren't moving to a single force then the band would not have voted to disband. It was premature to throw in the towel. As I understand it, Neil Hall, the then Pipe Major, had taken a job in Dubai and a lot of people left when he decided to go. But you don't know what's going to happen in the future. If the band remains disbanded then Edinburgh won't have a contribution to make and that is sad."

Even although they were stressful times, Colin enjoyed his time in charge at Fettes. "I had great fun with the band. It was a real challenge and one that I think was met quite successfully in that we got the band back into Grade 1. Nobody thinks the pipe major of a Grade 1 band is a magician. You have to have the players. You can do all the teaching and training and encouraging you want but you need to have the players. I was able to bring some people into the band and the practices were good. We had success in Grade 2 and some relative success in Grade 1."

Success in Grade 1 is, according to Colin, not easy to come by. "Grade 1 is a very tough environment and we got there. I think we had a seventh and we were broken on ensemble for a prize, it would have been the first prize the band would have won in decades. The will and commitment to get from that eighth, ninth, or tenth place up into the prize list was a huge jump and the guys found it difficult. I mean, pipe bands are largely made up of what we would call amateur players or hobbyists and the work required to crack the prize list is really a full-time job."

A full-time job that has been helped to a certain extent by improvements in technology since Colin started playing, although some of these improvements are perhaps now being shunned. "There is a lot of talk about technological improvements but a lot of the top bands have gone back to the same materials they were using years ago in the seventies, with cane reeds and sheepskin bags. Now you have bands going back to using Sinclair chanters. I'm not sure the instrument has improved dramatically. It might have improved in terms of getting it going but the whole business of getting a sound probably hasn't been made any easier."

MacLellan does believe that advances in technology in other areas have helped the pipe band world evolve. "People are flying all over the world to play in Grade 1 bands. Air travel now is pretty affordable and so it's easier for people to decide they want to play with bands on the other side of the world. When we grew up in Edinburgh your ambition had to be to play in the Edinburgh Police Pipe Band. But because there wasn't another band to play with, apart from Woolmet & Danderhall and Bilston Glen who were a bit out of Edinburgh, and because Edinburgh Police were looking for serving police officers, folk from Edinburgh started looking farther afield and people started going elsewhere, but the expenses and time involved in travel meant that options were pretty limited. Now people can choose to play in a band in New Zealand and you have people from Canada playing in bands in Scotland and all over the place. I think to make all that worthwhile the whole level of the pressure to succeed and the commitment needed has got much greater. The prize money hasn't increased much but what it means to win the Grade 1 World Championship most certainly has."

A Piper's Tale

There is no doubt that winning the Worlds is one of the biggest prizes in piping, as others have commented on in these pages. For MacLellan it is a great thing for Glasgow as well as piping. "I think it's destined forever now to be in Glasgow as long as the whole concept of Piping Live! works. I think it is fair that it is in Glasgow and I don't think anyone has a problem with that, particularly since it is a quality event. It's difficult to justify it being anywhere else right now because I don't think anybody else is an a position to offer what that city is offering and that's why there is less of a clamour for it to be moved. It is a great event and one of the big boosts for piping is that Scotland, and Glasgow Council, have started to realise what a big event it is and how much money it brings in to the country and the city. It's hard to imagine any events in Scotland bigger than the World Pipe Band Championship, apart from maybe a cup final."

For Colin it's not just the World's that is important but the fact that it is now so closely associated with Piping Live! which has been filling the streets and concert halls of Glasgow with great piping in the week leading up to the Worlds for ten years now. "It's tagged on at the end of Piping Live!, and that's been a fantastic thing for piping as well. And it's on TV. I remember when I was working at The Edinburgh Academy and the head of music at the primary school, a wonderful woman called Margaret Donaldson, came in one morning and said, 'Oh Colin, do you know I watched this programme last night about the World Pipe Band Championship.' She is a very accomplished musician and she was amazed. She said she had no idea that bagpipes could play like that and that it was exceptional as a musical instrument. So the TV coverage is bringing the instrument to other pipers and to the public, and that's why the pipes are now cool. There was none of that happening when we were growing up and it's awful nice to see it happening now."

Roddy MacLeod

Roddy MacLeod and his brothers started to learn the pipes at the same time, not long after the family moved to Cumbernauld, which was still a town very much in its infancy, in the early sixties. "I have a memory of my dad getting a set of Hardie pipes and coming back to the house with them and of the family pet, a Shetland collie, howling as my dad tried to blow the pipes. He could get a tune out of the practice chanter, partly by ear and partly by instruction. I'm not sure how patient he was, but he was certainly keen for us to learn. My older brother Calum was about twelve and Colin was three years older than me, and they were both getting into chanter lessons. At the same time my sister Fiona was going to Highland dancing, so the will was there for us to get involved in that kind of thing. I was going along initially as an observer since it was easier to pack the three of us off to our teacher Willie Campbell's house in Kildrum. I would get a bit of cake and a diluting orange, and I suppose it was natural that I would want to try to have a wee bash at it as well."

Roddy learned his first tunes in the Cumbernauld Caledonia Pipe Band with Hugh Wilson. "I think I was able to pick it up quite quickly because I had learned a bit from my brothers — how to play a birl and a D throw for example. Hugh corrected what needed to be corrected and gave me some exercises, and the Logan's Tutor. I think the first tune that Hugh taught me was the 'Quaker's Wife', a simple little march, and then there would be tunes like 'Land of My Youth'. That was where it started. Then we went to Glasgow with the family when I was about twelve and I didn't really know what to do about my piping. I suppose everything is up in the air in these situations — you are starting a new school and you have to think what to do. When I started my new school it turned out that one of the teachers played the pipes and I could hear him playing in his room at lunchtime. He put me in touch with a couple of boys in the school who were going along to the Glasgow Schools Pipe Band and so I got involved in that. Duncan Campbell was the piper and he was also going along to the College of Piping and so I followed him along there. I quickly thereafter started to get lessons from Duncan Johnstone. That was kind of it. I got involved in the College and had lessons from various teachers, Duncan Johnstone in the main but also Duncan MacFadyen and Angus MacLellan."

Competition soon followed for Roddy. "I started playing in competition when I was about thirteen or fourteen. The first one was at Glasgow Academy. It was an annual schools competition for private schools. I wasn't at a private school but they had an open competition that you could enter and being in the Glasgow Schools' Pipe Band I did exactly that. I remember practicing quite hard for that and got 2nd prize playing the '25th KOSBs'. Donald MacLeod was judging."

It was this first competition that really spurred the young Roddy MacLeod into action. "After that I just got the bug. I can't remember who I competed against but as the next year or two progressed then obviously it would be the likes of Ian Plunkett and Kevin Moffat. They were both involved in the Red Hackle Pipe Band which I subsequently joined. A year or two ahead of me would be others like Wilson Brown and a very good piper from Oban, taught by Ronnie Lawrie, called Neil Johnstone. Doing well down in Argyllshire, even although I didn't run into him until a year or two later, was Willie McCallum. I started to do quite well in the junior scene and progressively started to pick up more prizes, and when I was eighteen I decided to take the plunge into playing in the open."

Open competition was a different animal in those days and Roddy has fond memories of early success, in romance as well as in music. "When you went into the open it really was open, a free-for-all where there were no grades. We would go round the games and competitions and you could be competing against the very best guys. I picked up a few prizes here and there but my first big prize was when I was about twenty years old and I won the overall prize in what was then known as The Edinburgh Police Competition, which was a two-day event."

"It was the first time Margaret had come to a competition with me and she bravely sat through the whole pìobaireachd event. Can you imagine that as a nice way to start a romance? She's not doing it these days, I can tell you. She was obviously trying to impress me. What always sticks in my mind about that one was that at the end I asked her how she thought I sounded and she said that she thought I had played well but that there was another man there, small in height, who she thought was really good. Turned out she was talking about Iain Morrison who had been one of my boyhood piping idols. Anyway, the result came out and I won the pìobaireachd and had done sufficiently well in the light music - I think I won the jig and a prize in the March, Strathspey and Reel - to win overall. That was a seminal moment for me, where I realised that I was recognised as a serious contender."

Roddy MacLeod

As Roddy suggests, the lack of a grading system meant that he was competing against some of his boyhood idols. "There were the likes of Iain Morrison, Pipe Major Angus MacDonald, Donald MacPherson, Hugh McCallum, Iain MacFadyen and Murray Henderson. These were all guys that I would have looked up to at that time. I guess it's much more incremental in its way today. In my early days you had to take the view that if you were going to compete you couldn't limit your horizons just because you're put in with the best. You've got to think that you can achieve the impossible dream of beating the people you think of as the gods of piping as you are growing up. You're chucked in against them and unless you are just going to pack up and go away you have to believe that you have a chance against them. It became a reality that day in Edinburgh that I could compete against them. At the time I thought that maybe I was lucky, maybe they all had an off day, maybe if I keep practicing I'll be okay. There was no point getting big headed because I knew I still had a lot to learn."

By this time Roddy had finished his degree and was doing some a teacher training course at Jordanhill College in Glasgow with a view to pursuing a full-time career in teaching, although he did look at options that would allow him to play bagpipes for a living. "At that time it was only with the Army or police that you seemed to be able to follow a full-time career and I did consider the police, but I'm colour blind so that was ruled out. I did consider the Army as well when I was younger because I thought, being young and naïve, that I might be able to play the pipes all day every day. I remember having a discussion about it with my father. He was keen for me to have a good university education and follow that route. I did a degree in maths and economics and at the end of my degree I had no idea what I wanted to do. I did the 'milk round' as they called it in those days, when lots of different employers came to university. I had just turned seventeen when I started university and did a three year ordinary degree so I was still only nineteen when I graduated, then I did a year at Jordanhill not knowing what I wanted to do. I did a year's teacher training thinking that if nothing came up I would have teaching to fall back on. I finished the course in June 1983 and started teaching maths two weeks before my twenty-first birthday. I was very young and I'm sure there are millions of people at that age who don't have a clue what they want to do. I quite enjoyed it actually and did it for thirteen years."

As well as starting to achieve some serious success in the solo competition world, Roddy was also spending a lot of time in the world of pipe bands. "The Red Hackle was my first venture into the serious pipe band world. I'd been in the Glasgow Schools' Pipe

Band but that was a learners' band and wasn't really competing, so the Hackle was a good place for me to learn. It had come off the back of a successful period with John Weatherstone. When I joined Malcolm MacKenzie had just taken over as pipe major and he had a lot of good players, and a very good young drum corps as well. I stayed in that a few years. Kevin Moffat and Ian Plunkett were in the band and I was also competing against them. They were established and were doing well so I suppose they gave me something to measure my performance against. We tried to keep up with each other's standards. I used to go to the Pipers Club at the Dorchester Hotel on a Thursday night so I could go along and have a tune. I got to know some of the guys who were in the British Caledonian Airways Band, guys like Ronnie McShannon and Tom Johnstone. I became aware of just how good the standard of piper in that band was and it looked like it was going places, so I became enticed to join them."

Another great thing about that band was the travel. "The band at that time was sending people all over. There were jobs anywhere in the world that British Caledonian Airways flew to. I think we got paid a bit of an allowance as well as food and accommodation and it was always a good laugh. You were looked after and would stay in the same place as the airline housed its cabin crew and staff, always good quality. The band used to go to Stonemount Highland Games in Atlanta, and going to Italy also became a bit of a feature. The first week I was in the band I got a call to ask me to go to Rio. My problem was I was a teacher and I couldn't ask for time off all the time. I didn't travel as much as some, but we flew to London every weekend to practice. Going away with a pipe band is always a good laugh, especially with the stories that do the rounds when the guys come back, and it was a great time to be in that band. There were a lot of great characters, and so many great pipers like Pipe Major Angus MacDonald, Allan MacDonald, Ronnie McShannon, and Joe Wilson. I'm sure I'm missing lots of people out."

Pipe bands aren't all about travel and a good laugh. Roddy MacLeod spent nearly twenty years as a playing member and ten years a pipe major of one of the top bands in the world, the Scottish Power Pipe Band and he reckons that the success of any band is about more than the ability of the pipers that make up that band. "I think it depends on who is leading. You might have a band of very good pipers but if you don't have the right person to lead them then they might end up rubbing everyone up the wrong way and it won't work. Having said that, there are several cases of where it worked very well. Muirhead & Sons Pipe Band is a great example. It did work because they won something like five World Championships under Bob Hardie and had a great bunch of players. The same with Strathclyde Police. People used to say that you couldn't get solo pipers to play together but they won the Worlds eleven out of twelve years and look at the pipers they had in their ranks. They had a fantastic pipe major and a very high calibre of piper with the opportunity to mould them into shape with their practice regime. Good pipers want to be good. They want the band to be good, but the attitude and frame of mind each player adopts and their commitment to the band is just as important as their ability. Nowadays the top bands are jam packed with good solo pipers."

Latterly Roddy MacLeod took on the job of managing Spirit of Scotland Pipe Band for its special appearance in the World Pipe Band Championships a few years ago. It wasn't the same as being in charge at Scottish Power. "Spirit of Scotland was really easy to manage; people wouldn't believe how easy. Having said that, having the self-confidence to lead practices in that kind of company was difficult. Even although I had known everybody individually, and had known them for years, to sit down and lead a practice with them was tough. There was a real twinge of nervousness to it but that disappeared because they all subscribed to the team spirit. In some ways it might have been easier than Scottish Power because nobody that was part of the set up wanted to be thought of as having an ego bigger than anyone else. Any comments that were made were helpful and made in a constructive way. Although on the face of it they are similar circumstances they are actually quite different. With Scottish Power, we had been competing at five majors and a few other competitions in a year and it's such a competitive focus. The band was getting to the very top level because we won Cowal and were the first non-Irish band to win the All-Ireland Championship. We were looking to get to the next level. After ten years of being in that environment with a lot of the same guys then you are not so inhibited at shouting your instructions or venting your frustration. With the Spirit of Scotland the most we had been together was a week and there was lots of mutual respect. I don't think we were going to start barking orders at someone who has won two Gold Medals and four Silver Chanters or something like that. There is no need for it anyway. I guess in 2008 we were in a much different environment and we just needed to call for their complete concentration and a team effort."

While he was a student, Roddy found his piping a welcome diversion from studying, but now he wishes he had fewer diversions. "Today, I wish I had more time to practice. I would really love to have a few weeks off and get my teeth into it. I do need to practice and in an average week my practice will vary depending on the time of year. If there's an important competition coming up I'll play every night and would normally do an hour on the pipes. I do also teach two or three hours in a day so my fingers are moving and if I have good students then they may even be playing some of the same tunes as the ones I've entered for the light music competitions, so I'm practicing them while I work."

Routine is important to Roddy when he practices. "My routine depends on the competition. For example, take The Glenfiddich where you have six marches, six strathspeys, six reels and six pìobaireachds to get through. You can't play all of that in one go. What I would do is to start off with a bit of light music with a couple of marches to get the fingers and pipes going and then maybe a strathspey and reel and then a complete MSR. I maybe go through three or four of the MSRs so that the pipes are ready for the pìobaireachd. I'd then probably tackle a ground and variation of one pìobaireachd, and then typically play one through from start to finish and round it off with the remaining MSRs. To keep myself happy I'd finish by playing a few hornpipes and jigs. That would easily take up my hour, in fact probably a bit more. However, there's always the complication of the bagpipe and it not sounding to your satisfaction."

If something is not to Roddy's liking with his bagpipe then that takes priority. "You can't leave that until the last second. I always feel that I need to try to get the pipes going so that they're going to their optimum a few days in advance, and then I don't have to be worrying about them. It doesn't always work out like that. You can't enjoy it to the same extent if your pipes are not sounding the way they should. If the instrument is distracting me then I'm not thinking about the music and I don't feel ever satisfied at the end of a practice. I really have to try to get them going in good order to get the most out of a practice."

A great-sounding bagpipe is one of Roddy MacLeod's strengths and people travel from far and wide to hear what is almost universally recognised as one of the best sounds around. "I got my pipes when I was about twenty. I had been playing a set of Glen pipes but there was a hairline crack on the middle drone tuning pin that I had repaired, but I didn't think it had worked that well, so I decided to keep my eye out for a new set. I managed to get my hands on an old Lawrie set, silver and ivory mounted. When I put that set of drones against a Naill chanter I had been playing from a couple of years earlier, and still play, the whole sound changed. I don't know what it was; maybe the resonance of the new drones, but the sound just seemed to come alive. I got them from John

Burgess who had this ability to source old pipes. I met him at Perth station and took them home to have a trial with them but I didn't need much time to know that these were the pipes I wanted. I did a sort of part-exchange. I gave him the set of Hardie's that my dad played and my dog used to howl to and the rest in cash. It was a lot of money in those days because I was a student but they have paid for themselves over and over again."

These are the pipes that Roddy MacLeod still plays today. "It became obvious that the bottom section of the bass drone had a bore that was too wide. They were a 1907 set and when you think about it the pitch would have been much lower at that time and they would have wanted to tune higher, but with a modern chanter the bass drone wanted to tune too low down. With the wide bore it kind of gurgled so I got a Hardie bottom joint and that was part of the transformation of the sound because it gave the bass drone a resonance, a depth and a buzz that it didn't have. You have the resonance of the tenors and the depth of the bass and it really brings the chanter alive, particularly the high A which has a real ring to it."

The other thing that obviously makes a difference to the sound is the sheepskin bag and the reeds that Roddy plays. "I've never gone down the synthetic route, apart from with a band set-up for a couple of years. I played one set with the band and one for solos from time to time but it's quite a lot of work to keep both so I mostly just played the one or just plonk in a different chanter or change the drone reeds. I've had pipe chanter reeds that have lasted me four or five years. I used to use McAlister reeds and when they sold their business to Jimmy Troy I switched to them. Young Jamie Troy was over in the summer and I got half a dozen reeds from him and told him that, with any luck, they would do me for the rest of my playing life. The chanter reed I wouldn't change often and I really try to look after that. The tenors are synthetic Eezydrone so I change them from time to time in order to maintain steadiness and reliability. I still use a cane bass drone reed, largely because I have yet to find a synthetic reed that works well in my bass drone. The Eezydrone tenor reeds work fine and they are easier to work with than cane."

Roddy also reckons that the pitch of his chanter has helped his overall sound, although he does sound a word of warning for pipers and pipe bands who want to play with other musicians. "The chanter I have is about thirty years old and it must have been quite bright in comparison to others at the time. Maybe that's why it seemed to stand out. It's right at the pitch that people seem to be happy playing at today. There are two scales people refer to, but in a warm environment it's up to pitch at about 454Hz or 480Hz depending on what meter they're using, and that's right where people would say that the modern pitch is. I wouldn't like to see bands going any higher than they are currently but people have probably been saying that for years. It's getting to the stage that if they go any higher they will be getting detached from other musicians. It doesn't really matter if it's a pipe band playing on its own but it they're looking to play with other musicians then I think they've gone as high as they can."

Although the pipe band pitch is, as far as Roddy Macleod is concerned, as high as it should go, the sound keeps getting better, even as the size of modern bands exceeds every expectation. "I honestly feel that the quality and the unison that pipe bands have is better than it's ever been. The sound that bands like Simon Fraser University, Field Marshal Montgomery and Scottish Power are producing is very tight and it's incredible to think they're doing that with twenty-five pipers. I always remember Strathclyde Police Pipe Band coming over the hill at Bellahouston and people said 'Here comes the big tank now', and they had something like twelve pipers. You look at these bands now and they've got seven or eight pipers across the front rank and they are maybe three or four ranks deep. The whole technology of tuning, the reliability and consistency of reeds and the way the band chanters are being produced with new CNC lathes technology, is obviously playing its part in making the togetherness of the sound more achievable. Unfortunately that technology hasn't done anything for the fingers yet."

Roddy has no problems with his fingers at the moment but he is enough of a realist to recognise that it's not all as easy as it used to be. "I guess there's no doubt, being thirty years older, that you need a bit more limbering up. I'll continue to compete as long as I can continue to get prizes at the top level."

Recent competition wins would perhaps lead many to think that Roddy has a fair bit of time to go yet before he needs to be making any decisions. "My most recent Glenfiddich win was a huge high for me because I felt that I hadn't been hitting the spot with my march, strathspey and reel playing but had a healthy record in the pìobaireachd section. I took a different approach and decided to talk to someone at the National Piping Centre and take advantage myself of the top level teaching that is available. I spoke to Stewart Samson, who is an excellent player with lots of experience. He has directed the Army School of Piping, he's the same age as me so there's no age barrier, and he's probably the one that was most likely to tell me what he really thinks. He picked up on a couple of things on my reel playing. It was a bit too fast and not strong enough on some of the accents. To be honest it was easier to fix than I thought it would be and it seemed I was probably trying to be more adventurous than I needed to be. So to win the MSR right after that was great because it came after three days of real hard work. I came off stage and thought I had played really well and was very happy with my performance, although I didn't know I would win. I was really pleased to hear my name come out and to win the MSR and the Overall Championship for the fourth time."

Hamish Moore

Hamish Moore's individual take on music began to develop when he was working, without much enthusiasm, as a veterinary surgeon in Ireland. "In the summer of 1981, after leaving veterinary practice and just prior to taking up a post with the Ministry of Agriculture, I travelled over to Milltown Malbay in west Clare to do a locum in a large animal practice; the work was mainly TB and Brucella testing. The people were unbelievably friendly. There were traditional music sessions in the pubs and it was here that I learned of the famous Willie Clancy Week of Music held every July in the town. So, fired with enthusiasm, accompanied by three of my friends and with a tin whistle in my pocket, I set off the following July to take whistle lessons and experience the magic of this truly amazing Irish festival. It was during this trip that I heard the likes of Liam O'Flynn, Paddy Maloney, Paddy Keenan and Joe McKenna playing tunes in the bars round Milltown."

When Hamish returned home to Scotland he felt that there had to be a Scottish equivalent to the uillean pipes. "I was recounting tales of west Clare to my friend and neighbour in Kingussie, John MacRae. John and his father before him were excellent pipers, but nothing prepared me for what I was to encounter on my kitchen table when I came downstairs for breakfast the following morning. John, in the middle of the night, had snuck in and left a pipe case on my table and in it was an early 19th century set of Scottish small pipes. By this time the bellows blown pipe revival had already started in Scotland and Jimmy Anderson was working with the likes of Rab Wallace, Dougie Pincock and Iain MacDonald of the Neilston and District Pipe Band in developing small pipes as well as Border pipes."

There was, however, a parallel but separate piece of work going on in Northumberland with Colin Ross, The Northumbrian pipe maker. "Colin had developed a Scottish small pipe chanter in the key of 'D' and his brother in law, Artie Tresize, had already incorporated this into the early days of their now world-famous The Singing Kettle show. It was to Colin that I turned to carry out the restoration work on my pipes and to make a new chanter in 'D' for them. I well remember the day I strapped the pipes on for the first time and started to make music with them. By the afternoon word had spread round the village and folk gathered to listen but also to play with me on this new instrument. I knew in my heart that this was a very significant day in my life, knew that somehow it was life-changing, but didn't as yet realise just what was in store for the future. For the first time I had found a social context for the pipes that made sense and somehow rang true for my cultural heart."

It also rang the bell on Hamish's time as a vet. "I had been granted four months leave of absence without pay that summer of 1986 because it was felt that 'it would hopefully get all this music out of his system and when he came back he would settle down and become a diligent Ministry vet'. Nothing could have been further from the truth, because when I returned at the beginning of October I immediately handed in my notice, worked the required three months, and finished with veterinary medicine for ever on the last day of December 1986."

"I started playing with a couple of local bands and incorporated the small pipes into the line-up of guitar and flute in one and clarsach, fiddle and tenor banjo in another. I met the wonderful band, Jock Tamson's Bairns, and was invited after their demise to play with three of their members, Iain Hardy, John Croall and Rod Paterson in the band Corda. Through my work in organising The Newtonmore Folk Club and subsequently The Festival, I met Dougie MacLean who invited me in 1985 to record my first album, Cauld Wind Pipes. This record was the first to feature the small pipes, the Border pipes and the pastoral pipes of Scotland. From this beginning I have had many wonderful experiences and adventures in a life involved in music, the arts and musical instrument making."

One of these experiences came after hearing a BBC Radio Four interview with our celebrated artist, John Bellany. "I had been aware of Barga in Tuscany and heard tale of its amazing connection with the West of Scotland with all the Italian immigrants settling in Largs, Saltcoats, Paisley and the Glasgow area in general. I had no idea just what a vast phenomenon this was until I heard John speak so eloquently of it. I made a mental note, 'I must get over there to see what this place is all about'; and so I did, in May 2007. I made the trip to Pisa and then on up through Luca and the Serchio valley to the walled mediaeval hill town that is Barga."

He was captivated. "Not only is it stunningly beautiful, but it is full of Scots Italians, many of whom have 'come home' and opened successful businesses in the town, and many others who simply visit friends and family on a regular basis. Sitting in certain piazzas at eight in the evening in the summer is like walking down Sauchiehall Street on a Saturday afternoon; at least linguistically it is. It is actually estimated that sixty percent of the town's population have relatives in the West of Scotland."

As often happens with life's adventures, this trip turned out to be much more than a holiday for Hamish. "I made friends with the man who was the artist, photographer and editor of the local online newspaper, Barganews. I chatted extensively with him about Barga, life, the arts, and particularly the concept of the 'artist in residence', something we both understood well and were very keen on. To précis a long story, within a couple of days he had arranged a meeting with the assistant mayor and I had been invited to be a guest of the town as artist in residence for the year, 2008. Without hesitation, but with not without a little trepidation about the ensuing adventure, I packed the back of my car with a lathe and all the other necessary equipment to go and work in Italy for a year. I crossed the Alps in the snow with half a workshop in the back of my car and after unloading in Barga set about making a studio for myself in one of the most beautiful piazzas in the world."

"One of the unique features of Barga, and the one which captured my imagination more than any other, is the fact that the town's streets are too narrow for cars and so the normal mode of getting from A to B in the town is by Shank's pony. The town is full of musicians, writers and artists and so on a daily basis, and in fact several times a day, it is very likely that I would bump into some very like-minded person who would, at the drop of a hat, stop for a coffee, go off for lunch, or simply share a glass of local wine. It is quite simply a blissful way to live."

The Italians have their own bagpipes as well of course, the zampogna, and Hamish managed to learn as much as he could from their masters while he was in Barga. "One of the highlights, amongst so many, of my year there was to be invited by The Italian Bagpipe Association to teach at their spring school in Isernia. It was a wonderful meeting, and associations and life-long friendships were made. After the teaching weekend, Duillio Viglotti from the Italian Bagpipe Association had arranged a trip to Scapoli, the centre of Italian zampogna making. It was fascinating to see the pipe makers at work and to hear of the latest developments and innovations to reach this ancient instrument. I also learned first-hand how lunch should be served; with many, many courses, copious quantities of fresh young Italian red wine, and singing and playing of pipes between, and as a part of, every course of their wonderful food. They know how to enjoy their music and food with not an element of guilt. We, as Scots, have a lot to learn in these matters."

Hamish Moore's Italian experiences make up a very important part of his musical life, but he believes that we need to look in another direction to discover more about our own musical heritage, and stop the damage that is currently being done to it. "One of the most important places in terms of cultural identity for Scotland is that of Cape Breton Island in Nova Scotia. It is here that many of the mysteries and enigmas of our culture are answered and explained. It was in 1986 at The Philadelphia Folk Festival where I first encountered a music which would change my life and eventually answer many of the questions I had concerning Highland music and its associated culture. I had heard tapes of music from Cape Breton but nothing would prepare me for the experience of hearing and feeling it in a live setting. I stood for a long time, listening and knowing that this was so meaningful and had a deep significance. It took several minutes to realise that what I was hearing was old Scottish music and old Highland pipe tunes, but played in a way that was unimaginably beautiful and vital, played like I had never heard before. Cape Breton is many things to many people and has caused much controversy within Scotland since its emergence back on our shores."

To understand that controversy, and the part that Cape Breton music plays in Hamish's story, it is important to understand his early life in piping. "My great-great-grandfather and my great-grandfather both played pipes, and my father was my first teacher. I was lucky enough at school in Edinburgh to have an excellent teacher, namely Jack Crichton, who tutored our school pipe band. I competed moderately successfully in solo piping competitions and became pipe major of the school pipe band. Jack, who was also in charge of Knightswood Juvenile band in Glasgow, invited me to guest with them, and this also helped in me attaining an exacting standard of playing. I went on in my last year at school to play for a Grade 1 band and carried on with this for one term after I started university in Edinburgh."

By this point, Hamish was struggling with the concept of competition, and the part it had played in changing our culture. "I was searching for a more musical approach to piping than I was finding in the competition system. The first piping competition was held in Falkirk at the end of the 18th century during the period when the Highland regiments were being raised. These two events, and what emerged as a result, were to change the face of piping beyond recognition. Piping had been a true oral tradition. Individual regional, as well as personal, styles were celebrated and encouraged. What followed was the antithesis of the approach to this ancient living culture. Competition came to demand technical excellence and as this improved more and more technique was added and applied to the already standardised settings of pipe music. The effect on the music was catastrophic as it became divorced from its original context. Technique and technical excellence came to dominate the way tunes were played and the rhythmic structure of the tunes became distorted. More rules were laid down by the now very powerful official organisations and governing bodies, and status and power in piping could only be gained by the winning of competitions."

In essence, according to Hamish, we had forgotten how to play our music. And it wasn't only our music that was affected. "In dance music we had forgotten how to play for the dance and we had forgotten the dance, the hard shoe percussive step dance of Scotland."

"I enrolled with the university country dancers and started playing for them. It was good fun, and very exacting and demanding from the rhythmic point of view. I enjoyed the challenge and they invited me every summer to travel to various folk dance festivals in Europe. Apart from the enjoyment of travelling abroad at that age and meeting so many lovely people, it in itself provided the focus for what was to become for me the symbol of the mystery of Scottish cultural identity. Why, I asked myself, did all the European groups turn up in peasant or quasi-peasant costumes but the Scots arrived with the women wearing white Victorian ball gowns complete with upper arm length white gloves and the men in black bow ties and the rest of the formal evening wear associated with the balls of high society London and Edinburgh. Every strand of our culture was to be classicised and formalised apart from what was held on to in the social and geographical fringes of Scotland. Our culture was to be changed so as to become unrecognisable from its original."

Then the Cape Breton link appeared. "It wasn't until Cape Breton was 'discovered' that we gradually were able to unearth this unique forgotten gem and what it was to offer Scotland. When it was suggested by Mary Janet MacDonald, who attended one of the early Barra fèisean, that the step dance as enjoyed in Cape Breton had originated in Scotland there were varying reactions. Farquhar MacRae, a dancing master from Barra, immediately knew that this was the case, whereas many others were sceptical. Farquhar had, in his attempt to piece together this mystery, come up with the concept of Hebridean Dancing but it was still quite 'Highland' and obviously, by his own admission, wasn't the full story. It wasn't until Maggie Moore of Birnam was teaching step dance in Fife one Saturday afternoon that we gathered the corroborative evidence required. Sheila MacKay, a seventh generation dancing master who was also involved in the dance workshop, rushed up to Maggie and demanded to know where she had learned her steps, to which

Maggie replied, 'Oh, that's Cape Breton step dancing'. Not only had Sheila never heard of Cape Breton but she then proceeded to dance the steps and confirm that the steps Maggie was dancing were the old steps handed down to her from her father. These had come down through the generations of her family. Maggie had learned the steps from the celebrated dancer from Cape Breton, Harvey Beaton, whose family were, like so many Cape Bretoners, from South Uist. When questioned as to why she no longer danced the steps, Sheila's response was both tragic and telling. The official Highland dancing organisation to which she belonged had made her feel ashamed of the steps."

Hamish knows that the same fate has befallen other musicians. "When the principal of the College of Piping in Glasgow visited Cape Breton in the 1950s to run a week-long piping course, half of the pipers put their pipes in their cases at the end of that week and never played them again, such was the shame they felt by being ridiculed about their style of playing. If only that principal had had the insight to know that he was so privileged to have witnessed the last generation of players on the planet who were playing in a true folk style. They had been preserved from the modern competitive style by generations of isolation and being free from the shame of celebrating their own Gaelic culture. They passed their playing down from generation to generation after leaving the Highlands of Scotland and it was rhythmically anchored by the dance which never lost its status as a vital part of their cultural identity. He had witnessed a true jewel in the crown of Gaelic culture and because of his prejudice hadn't even been aware of it. I was privileged to know the very last living exponent of this way of playing, Alex Currie from Cape Breton, and I can confirm that his style of playing was fundamentally so radically different from modern competition piping as to be unrecognisable as having come from the same tradition."

Hamish reckons we have a lot to thank Cape Breton for. "Quite simply, amongst all the various and many gifts given so openly and freely by our Cape Breton cousins, the most precious are these; they gave us our dance back and they gave us our way to play for it. This seems to me to be of monumental importance to a culture searching for its true identity. They also gave us a way of appreciating our music, filled with joy and love and unfettered by the competitive jealousies surrounding competition. As importantly, they have given us an exuberant enthusiasm for, and awareness of, our own Gaelic culture and language. Quite simply, they held our dance and its accompanying style of music in trust for us. What a unique gift."

Dougie Pincock

Dougie Pincock never intended to learn the pipes. It was an accident brought about by a combination of lack of success on other instruments and two men's desire to have piping taught in schools. "Pipes were the fourth instrument that I had tried. My mother was desperate for me to learn the accordion and we found an old one that belonged to an uncle but we couldn't find anybody to teach me. As a primary school kid I wasn't savvy enough to figure it out for myself. I got a book and tried to figure out the chords but couldn't do it. My father had been a bit of a drummer in the Boys' Brigade and he showed me some basics with a set of sticks."

"I had the obligatory recorder lessons as well and I wasn't bad at that. The pipes were number four and they felt right. There was no tuition in Scottish schools at that time really, apart from Farquhar McIntosh, who later became Sue, and who was appointed in Inverness schools in 1969. Seumas McNeill was at the College of Piping and John MacFadyen was the head teacher at my school, Springhill Primary. They were on a bit of a crusade to get piping into the schools, and to this day I don't know where the budget came from, but John brought in a guy called John Garroway who had just retired from Glasgow Police, as it was at the time. He had been in the Glasgow Police Band in the fifties with Ronnie Lawrie, Charlie Scott and the MacDonald brothers from South Uist. "

When Dougie left primary school he went to lessons at the College of Piping and was taught by Angus MacLellan and Ronnie Lawrie. He also joined Neilston and District Pipe Band and met the guy who was to become one of the biggest influences in his musical life. "We have to talk about Iain MacDonald. Not because he taught me, because he didn't sit down and teach me tunes in the way that conventional teachers do, but what he did do was to introduce me to all sorts of people both within and without the world of piping, and to all sorts of types of music. Iain was quite ahead of his time. He had been the singer in a rock band that was playing round Paisley, a band called The Incision, and even at that stage in the mid-seventies, when he was in his mid-twenties, he had what seemed to me like an enormous record collection. He was always lending me stuff and I remember hearing Planxty and The Bothy Band. He was into uillean pipes early on for someone in Scotland and he had Seamus Innes and Felix Doran records, all that kind of stuff."

Iain had also played on a special Battlefield Band album featuring pipes from around the British Isles. "I thought I would quite like to do that and then I heard John Gahagan playing 'Lady Madelina Sinclair' and the 'Duke of Perth' on the tin whistle and I thought I would really like to do that. I would never have heard all of that if I didn't know Iain. This was happening about the same time as Alan MacLeod was playing with Alba, and he had been at the College of Piping at the same time as me. He was already the bad boy. Gordon Duncan gets credited with note bending and the 'C natural' but Alan MacLeod was into it in the early seventies with a tune called the 'Cook in the Kitchen'. We were all slightly in awe of him, even although he was only a couple of years older than us."

Dougie had been competing round the junior solo competitions but he stopped when he joined Glasgow band Kentigern. "I liked the music and I still play the music. I am happy that competitions exist and I'm happy for other people to play in them but when I found this thing called folk music, traditional music, call it what you will, it seemed to me to that this was the way that I wanted to play. It was the collaboration I liked. I had been finding it quite lonely out there competing. I used to get an awful lot of third or fourth prizes and by that time you're pretty much where you're going to be technically. Nothing much is going to change. I've never had a great competitive streak so it didn't really bother me if I didn't win, and it was becoming more like sport rather than music. It didn't feel right. I'd been playing at sessions in the Victoria Bar and the Third Eye Centre in Glasgow and getting a buzz that I just wasn't getting when I was on my own playing in competitions."

At the same time Dougie, keen to expand his musical knowledge, bought a G whistle and learned some of the tunes he had heard John Gahagan playing. That was when he realised how limited his general musical knowledge was. "In those days I had no idea what a key was. I thought a whistle was just a whistle. I went into the session in the Victoria Bar and told John I'd learned these new tunes and played them to him. He was killing himself laughing so he got a D Whistle out and told me about octaves and showed me how I should have learned them. My head nearly exploded when I heard all this."

Instead of this experience putting him off, Dougie was filled with enthusiasm to learn as much as he could about the music he wanted to play. "I was in the university Officer Training Corps Pipe Band and we were at a summer camp or training weekend. I was with this guy who played piano as well as pipes and he knew a bit about music. He sat down with a bit of manuscript paper and showed me how to make a major scale out of tones and semitones. He showed me that if you skip a note and go the next one and then skip another note and go to the next one, and if you do that three times, you end up with this thing called a chord, and it was great. I can't remember his name but I do remember all the things he taught me. I was basically still a piper playing a few tunes on the whistle, but I was learning."

Although he was deeply immersed in what he calls 'traditional music' by this point, he hadn't forgotten his piping, largely because he was spending time with the man who was the second big musical influence in his life. "Duncan Johnstone was a fixed thing that I kept returning to, he was like my North Star and I kept in touch with him right up until he died. He came to Neilston Pipe Band practices - which is how I first met him - and then when I was in my first couple of years at university me and my best mate would go to Duncan's house for a lesson and then a couple of pints afterwards."

"That went on for quite a while and I was still doing a little bit of competing. Then I went on the road in June 1983 with the Battlefield Band, and in breaks between tours I would still go to see him at least three or four times a year. Not necessarily to learn anything new but just to make sure I wasn't doing anything daft. He loved what I was doing with the Battlefield Band. He always thought of himself as a musician who played the pipes. He had a couple of nicknames. Most people know the King of the Jigs one but he hated that name because there was an implication that that was all he could do. Duncan was also a really good pìobaireachd player, he had learned from Bob Brown. He just didn't compete. He got very nervous competing, figured it wasn't worth it, and stopped. Because he didn't have a cabinet of medals and prizes he doesn't figure highly in some people's lists of significant pipers. He had another nickname that Seumas McNeill gave him and that was The Piper's Piper. That was much more like it."

Duncan Johnstone also supplied lots of tunes for Dougie and the other pipers who were playing with folk bands. "He was very supportive of me and of Iain MacDonald when he first joined Kentigern. Remember we are talking about the mid-seventies when there were very few pipers in folk groups. There was Alan MacLeod with Alba, Jimmy Anderson was playing with The Clutha, Rab Wallace was playing with the Whistlebinkies and that was about it. There wasn't a great repertoire for the pipers to play in these bands and most of us played Irish music since the competition 2/4 marches didn't really cut it. Iain went to Duncan who told him there were hundreds of these wee tunes lying around he could play and he pointed Iain to some of the older collections. A vast number of tunes came out of that, and Duncan was delighted to hear them being played again. He was also very generous with his own compositions. Lots of composers would be very guarded but Duncan was great and very free with his tunes. He always insisted that we didn't mess around with the tunes, 'Yes, by all means play my tunes, but please play them properly'."

Some of the pipers playing these tunes felt the need to get together with Dougie to record an album produced by Robin Morton from The Boys of the Lough, who was also a very well respected producer in his own right. "The Controversy of Pipers was a Robin Morton project and he was very perspicacious about these things. He was also the first guy to put out a record of Gaelic song with Flora MacNeil. He could see that people needed to know more."

"One of the problems that pipers playing in folk groups faced was the potential accusation from the establishment that you were playing folk music because it was all you could do, you couldn't play a march, strathspey and reel, or a pìobaireachd or whatever. That argument was current when Duncan MacGillivray was playing in Battlefield Band and Jimmy Anderson in the Clutha. The purpose of the album was to demonstrate that even though we were playing in folk groups we were good pipers and we could play properly. There was an element of demonstrating a breadth of repertoire as well. There were six pipers on the album. I played along with Iain MacDonald from Glenuig, Pipe Major Iain MacDonald from Neilston, Rab Wallace, Jimmy Anderson and Duncan MacGillivray. People forget that Rab Wallace was a very good competitive piper. Jimmy Anderson and Rab had played together at Muirhead's at a very high level in the pipe band world and Iain MacDonald was brought up in Queen Victoria School in Dunblane. We all had these strong backgrounds. There was some great music; some competition stuff, the Breton set that Iain MacDonald put together, some 4/4 marches, some wee strathspeys and reels and there's a pìobaireachd. It was the first time that 'Lament for Alan my Son' by Duncan Johnstone was recorded and played by Rab Wallace."

Dougie went to Glasgow University to study Civil Engineering when he left school. The full story of Dougie's time there is probably the subject of a whole new book, and is probably summed up best in the John Gahagan tune, 'Dougie's Decision'. Decision to leave that is, although not before he had wandered around several departments trying to find something that he enjoyed as much as playing music. "In 1981 I was involved in the house band in a play that Robin Morton was Musical Director for. I think people already knew that I was a piper who played traditional music but during the course of that job I displayed a bit of versatility. The band was Malcolm Jones of Runrig, a drummer called Dave Swanson, a keyboard player called Robert Pettigrew and a fiddler who also acted called Rab Hanley. The play, Capital Offence, was written by Hector McMillan who wrote The Sash. Hector had chosen the music and it included a lot of traditional tunes with contemporary arrangements. It was basically a rock band with me and Rab at the front of it. I had to be versatile, playing pipes and whistles. Duncan MacGillivray was trying to get out of Battlefield Band at the time and I think it was that job that really brought me to their attention, especially since Robin Morton was involved. Battlefield Band couldn't afford to have a piper who only played pipes and I think that job let Robin see my versatility. I was still at university so I would have tried not to describe myself as a full-time professional musician but I was spending more time playing music than studying. Malcolm Jones asked me if I had considered going professional and when I said no he said, 'Why not, you can play the bloody stuff'. That that was the first time I thought seriously about it."

The play was also paying good money, he was enjoying it and it was a great experience. "Shortly thereafter I got the offer from the Battlefield Band but I still had this feeling that I had an obligation to my parents to get a degree so I told them I was going to join the band after I had finished. Duncan kept my seat warm until then but I went on to fail not one but two degrees. The engineering thing didn't work out and Seumas McNeill who was, as well as being Principal of the College of Piping, a Lecturer in Natural Philosophy got me a switch over to the science faculty at the start of my fourth year in 1982, but by January 1983 I was out on my ear just waiting to join the Battlefield Band."

He remained a bit unsure about life on the road. "I had five months of doing gigs here and there to fill in the time but even though destiny was driving me in that direction I still wasn't sure about the full-time thing. That's where John Gahagan was really helpful. He had tried it himself and decided it wasn't for him but he told me, and it's a piece of advice I've passed on to lots of young folk since, 'Try it. If you don't try it you'll spend the rest of your life wondering what it might have been like'."

Dougie travelled the world ten times over playing with the Battlefield Band sharing the stage with some amazing musicians.

Dougie Pincock

He was helping to expose a whole new audience to the sound of the pipes along the way. "I wouldn't say I was advancing the cause of the bagpipe, that's maybe a bit bold, but what I think we were doing is that we were showing the possibilities of the instrument. We were showing pipers, and other people, that you could choose to do something else with the pipes. We didn't say 'We're going to do rock and roll songs and so should you', it was nothing like that, but we would do new things. We used the pipes in songs. A good example was a song of Brian's called 'The Roving Dies Hard' where we put a big pipe section in it. The pipes were a central part of it and I was proud of that."

It also produced the complement that Dougie is most proud of. "I was introduced a few years ago to Niall Vallely, the concertina player, and he said 'I know who this man is. I was in the Queen's Hall in Belfast and this guy came on the stage with the Battlefield Band and it was the first time I realised that the Highland bagpipe was a musical instrument.' That's coming from a guy who grew up in the North of Ireland in some of the worst times that the place has had and in a traditional Irish family. To a lot of these guys the bagpipe was a symbol of the other side. He'd never seen it being presented in any terms other than as part of a pipe band in a military context. I honestly think that if I never influenced anything else in my time as a musician I would have been happy with that one comment."

Dougie Pincock has influenced lots of other people, and has had some wonderful experiences along the way. There have been some strange and daunting ones as well. "The hardest thing I ever did was a radio play written by Don Paterson based on the idea that jazz was invented in Scotland rather than America and the iconic instrument of jazz rather than being the tenor saxophone was actually the accordion. Don put a band together for the play with a guy playing accordion sounds on a Synclavier, which was one of the early sampling keyboards. He called me up, asking what notes the pipes could play, so I told him about 'C natural' and the rest and that although it was difficult we could do it. He wrote tunes that were absolutely littered with these notes, and he sent me bits of it. Not a lot, eight or sixteen bars at most. I then went into the studio with three of the best jazz musicians in Europe, put the pipes up, played the eight bars, and stopped thinking that was the end of it. I asked why they were carrying on after we had played the tune and they said 'That's just the head. We just play it again and again and we each get a chance to improvise'. Well, I'd never done anything like that before."

Worse was to come when Dougie found out about his

character. "We were getting to the end of the session and Don came on the talkback and said 'Right, your character is a drug dealer and in this section he is on stage playing the pipes and his mobile phone goes and he has to answer it so you need to play this bit with one hand'. I had to take one hand off the chanter and play, still doing chromatic improvisations. Talk about a handicap."

Dougie also ended up playing on a CD recorded by Tom Tom Club, effectively Talking Heads without David Byrne, and it came about in the most surreal manner. "Tom Tom Club played dance music. Susie Petrov, the piano player, and I had done a house concert up in the woods in Vermont and one of the people there was a woman who lived a few doors away. She wanted to buy a tape but had no money so she came back the next morning and while we were talking we discovered she was Tina Weymouth's mother. Tina was the bass player in Talking Heads. I told her I was a big fan and she said Tom Tom Club were making a new album and we should go and play on it. I said I didn't think it worked that way but she said 'No, I'll call them and tell them'. She did. And they said 'Yes mum', and we did. We recorded a track in B flat and one in A and they used the A version. I turned up at the studio and they had a four bar loop of drums and bass. They told me to play over it for a while and they would take the bits they liked. So I played for six or eight minutes, just some bits of tunes and some improvised stuff. They were pleasantly surprised because they had no idea what to expect and Tina Weymouth, who wrote the lyrics, used some of my bits for the melody of one of the songs so I got a writers credit as well. The album is called Dark Sneak Love Action. There are ten tracks on it and I've got a one-tenth writer credit on one of the tracks so I've got a one-hundredth credit for which I have received the princely sum of $100 in royalties plus $400 for the session fee. That was all right."

All of these experiences were great fun and allowed Dougie to visit places and meet people that he would never otherwise have met, but he also believes that they have been instrumental in making his current job, as Director of The National Centre of Excellence in Traditional Music in Plockton, much easier. "Working with Van Morrison and sharing stages with Dr John and KD Lang couldn't but help. Anyone who could do all that and not learn anything doesn't deserve to be doing it. At the very least you can learn about musicianship, what other people are doing, and borrow some of these ideas and get experience. I use every single bit of it in the school. Because my role is mainly managerial, the contact I have with the students is usually in group work and I can talk about these experiences."

Dougie Pincock

Dougie, with no formal teaching qualification or knowledge of the education system, was not an obvious choice for the high profile appointment. "It's been a very steep learning curve and a lot of people have helped to make it all work. Putting a musician into this job was very brave, rather than a teacher or somebody with a background in education. They took a huge gamble with me and it could have backfired on them. I answered a lot of the criteria on the job spec and that is why I applied in the first place but they knew there was a colossal gap in my knowledge about the education system. I had to learn real quick. People like Laurence Young and Bert Richardson, who was an advisor in music, and the people at Plockton High School, Duncan Ferguson the Rector, and Donald Ferguson, one of the Depute Rectors at the time, were marvellous at enabling me to learn education speak . It was a steep ride as far as the managerial role and dealing with parents was concerned. My one rule is to assume that everyone is sincere and deserves a bit of respect and I take it from there. Sometimes I'm proved wrong, but very rarely."

His other experiences and skills also help when it comes to dealing with the students. "The advantage of dealing with kids is that I'm a parent. I don't tuck them in at night or pat their knee if they cut it, but I know how to deal with kids and I think about how I would want other people to treat my kids."

The National Centre of Excellence is helping to produce some great musicians but there are still those in the piping world who need to be convinced that involving the bagpipes in traditional music is a legitimate use of the instrument. "I'm not convinced the argument will ever be resolved. There will always be some people who think there is one way to play and some who think there is another. The situation has changed though. There is a growing number of people who are more tolerant, and a lot of the guys like Iain MacFadyen, who wasn't too impressed to begin with, are now behind it. Iain is very proud of the work he's doing here, and rightly so."

Iain was a natural choice for tutor. "When we first came up here we realised that Iain was on the doorstep and we weren't going to look for another tutor. I asked him if he was interested in doing the job and as it happened he was just about to retire from his local authority post so it suited him very well. He said right at the start that he would love to do it but that he would teach these people marches, strathspeys, reels and pìobaireachd because that is what he knows. If they want folk group piping or small piping then I would have to do it. That's how we do things, and a very satisfactory arrangement it is. It would be interesting to ask some of the kids to get their take, but that's how it works. He comes to the concerts and watches them. He likes it and tells other people about it. There are far more opportunities, because of what we have done, for people to play pipes in different places."

More different places for pipers to play, but more pipers being produced every year at Plockton, the National Piping Centre, The College of Piping and The Royal Conservatoire of Scotland. "There are far more outlets and that makes it easier but of course there are more pipers trying to do it. Go back to the Controversy of Pipers album when there were only the six of us trying to do it full-time and compare that to now."

"Are there too many being produced now? That's a fabulous question. I'll go with no, on the grounds that you can never have too many good musicians. From an artistic and cultural point of view, no. From a commercial point of view, if I was out there trying to make a living now, then yes, there are too many singers, fiddle players and guitarists. Places like us, the RCS, the National Piping Centre and the College are spitting out tremendous young musicians and that has improved since our day. But the audience hasn't grown in comparison; in fact it might have shrunk due to the economic situation. The way people consume the music has had a bit of an effect. People are downloading rather than buying CDs. I heard Bruce MacGregor the other week on BBC Scotland's Travelling Folk. Apparently he'd said something on Twitter about somebody coming up to him after a gig and asking where he could download the music for free. Bruce responded, asking why he should have to work for free. Music is available free now and people are having to work harder."

As well as working harder, Dougie also believes that pipers need to work, and think, more creatively. He believes, as he touched upon earlier, that competition and creativity are not natural bedfellows. "If you want to win a prize you have to play a certain way, especially if you are playing for a certain judge. You have to make sure you don't miss a single gracenote, that your pipes are perfect, and that will become your priority at that level no matter how good you are. I hear people talking about sound being the priority, then technique, then music, and that is just wrong. If music is not your priority, you won't experiment. You'll play safe, especially if you want to win a prize. Competition is the enemy of creativity in music. It keeps standards high but in the world of the pipe band it is the enemy of creativity. Some bands have managed very well to be creative in competition, but you have to be big enough and brave enough to know that it might not get you a prize. I think the world of the pipe band would explode with creativity if people stopped worrying about competitions. If more bands were allowed, or were brave enough, to do things like the National Youth Pipe Band are doing with backing musicians, then there would be an explosion of creativity ready to take place, but it's being stifled by the need to impress judges and win prizes. People need to be brave."

Finlay MacDonald.

Red Hot Chilli Pipers.

Roddy MacLeod and Willie McCallum share a dram or twa'.

Chris Armstrong.

Gordon Walker.

Murray Henderson.

Faye Henderson.

Iain MacFadyen.

The Battlefield Band.

Carlos Nuñez.

A young Fergus Muirhead, centre.

Terry Tully

Terry Tully's piping career has always been a family affair. "Both my father and mother were pipers. My father got involved in a pipe band called the Dublin City Girls' Pipe Band back in the late forties and that's where he met my mother. She was a piper in the band and he started teaching them around about that time. They got married in the early fifties and moved to the country where my father took up farming on a small farm. He had given up playing pipes at this point and put his career on hold for around ten years. When the novelty of farming life wore off they moved back to County Dublin, to Palmerstown, and it was then, in 1966, that I started to play. I started with the St Joseph's Pipe Band, based on the outskirts of Dublin, where my father was their instructor. I had my first lesson when I was about nine."

Terry's father wasn't content with one pipe band however, and Terry soon followed suit. "He was also pipe major of St Laurence O'Toole Pipe Band, (SLOT) having taken on that role in 1964. I joined SLOT in 1974 and at the time the band was in Grade 2, struggling at the bottom end. My father spent a lot of time sitting around a table teaching people and bringing them on to a level where they could play at the bottom end of Grade 2. It was in 1984 that he passed away suddenly and I had been pipe sergeant of the band for a number of years, so basically I was left the pipe major's job in my father's will. We built the band by going out and giving decent performances, getting noticed for the sound and the type of music that we played, by building the ranks, and by having people sitting round a table and being taught. It just grew from there."

Grow it certainly has. With a World Championship in Glasgow and several All-Ireland Championships under its belt, the band has become one of the major players in the world pipe band scene. "The present day band is made up of about forty-five playing members. We have ten pipers and two drummers from Northern Ireland, and four pipers from Scotland — three from Glasgow and one from Edinburgh. The balance of the band is people from Dublin and surrounding areas, and a few people from Arklow, Wexford. All over the place really."

This movement of players is a real feature of the modern pipe band and it's not without its issues when it comes to arranging practices. "The Scottish guys conduct their own practices in Glasgow on a weekly basis, and from September each year we organise Saturday practices where they take the opportunity to take cheap flights with Ryanair and come to Dublin once a month."

It's not only the players coming from Scotland who have to make a huge effort to get to practices. "There are people in our band from the North who will do their day's work, get into their car and travel for two and a half hours, do a two and a half hour band practice, then travel home for another two and a half hours. It's a huge commitment. I think that the reason they do it is partly because they've been involved in the band for quite a while - ten years or so for many of them - and it's partly because of the fact that they realise that the band has huge potential. It has the potential to win major competitions and to win another World Championship. I suppose it's easier for them to be getting into their car and driving to Dublin than hopping on a plane and travelling to Scotland."

It's not only a time commitment for the pipers and drummers travelling to Dublin. "Everybody in the band funds their own trip, even the pipers in Dublin and the North. This year it's five trips for the major championships, and we each pay for our own flights, accommodation, food and drink. We do this four or five times a year at our own expense. People often ask me where we are going on holiday. My answer is that I'm going to Scotland five times. How can I afford anything else?"

The practice, as well as the trips to Scotland, are certainly paying off and SLOT, as the band is almost universally known, is hitting some real high spots at the moment. "The highlight would have to be winning the Worlds. Before that it would be winning the All-Ireland Championships in Grade 1. To date we've won it three times since 2007. Up to that we've come close by maybe winning the medley and losing it on the MSR. I didn't want to have to retire as pipe major without having won our own national championships in Grade 1. After that it would have been winning our first major, the Scottish Championship in 2008 in Dumbarton."

It hasn't been an easy ride for Terry, but he always knew what the band was capable of. "Before my father died, I felt that the potential was there for the band to be a lot better than it was and with help of people like John Wilson and others I went down a different road to improve the band, because I knew it could be improved. We were getting better every year, that's what kept me going because I could see the fantastic potential and as it grew better in performance it attracted a better quality player. If you look back at the photos of the band twenty-five years ago there are only two of us left, me and Ronan Maguire. Since those early days there has been a huge turnover. What has kept me going is the realisation that the band has great potential and we could reach the ultimate of a World Championship. We did, and hopefully we can get to that point again."

As well as the improvements brought about by an increasingly high standard of players, Terry also recognises the help he has received from outsiders. "One man that I never had a lot to do with but whom I had the greatest respect for as a piper was Tom Anderson. I can remember that when he came to Ireland in 1972 or so he became the pipe major of St Patrick's band in Donnachmore. St Patrick's were a Grade 1 band in Northern Ireland who used to travel south to two or three competitions every year, and for me growing up as a boy and as a teenager, having the opportunity to listen to them when Tom was the Pipe Major, standing back in awe at how well they could sound, how well they could play together and the great music they played, it was all a great education. Tom Anderson would have been a big influence on me, and in the latter days we also got a lot from people like John Wilson and Jim Wark, particularly John because he was here more often. He parted with a lot of information in my early years as a pipe major and was very helpful to me even before that, when he came to Dublin several times and took some of us for individual tuition for MSRs and for solo playing."

Although these guys all made a big difference to Terry and helped him a lot in his early years, he looks closer to home for his greatest inspiration. "That would have been my father who started me playing in 1966. He was my biggest influence in music generally because he also played the accordion and traditional music and I suppose that's where the background of my traditional music came from."

Terry reckons that the background he has in the wider music of Ireland has helped him with the band, although perhaps not at first. "You could say that for a long time I personally made the mistake of playing the type of music that we wanted to play as opposed to playing the type of music that judges wanted to hear. Because of my background in traditional Irish music, and my father's background in traditional Irish music, there was always the tendency for the band to play a lot of that type of music. Whether people are of the opinion that traditional Irish music is more musical than traditional Scottish music, or the other way round, I don't know, but that's what we did. At times it didn't help the band that we played so much traditional Irish music, particularly in competition because, as I said, we played what we liked to play ourselves as opposed to what judges wanted to hear. We now have had a better cross section of music in the band in terms of what we play in competition where we mix the two traditions a lot better. We play a little bit of traditional Irish and some traditional Scottish and then we also play some modern contemporary music that could perhaps be composed by band members. That's what we have been doing in recent years and it seems to be going down a lot better with the judges"

In the world of competing pipe bands, pleasing the judges is what it's all about at the end of the day. "I think judges adopted the attitude that they saw us as a pipe band that had a bit of a reputation for playing traditional Irish music and that whenever we went out to play, whether we were playing traditional Irish, or traditional Scottish, or contemporary Irish, they still formed the opinion that we were playing traditional Irish music. It took a long time to get the point across that what we were playing, regardless of its origin, was music, and good music, and whether it came from one tradition or another didn't make any difference to us. It was what we wanted to play and it was what we liked to play, it didn't matter whether it was Scottish or Spanish or Breton or whatever."

Although SLOT are fairly recent winners of the World Championship, Terry Tully still thinks that the band has something to prove. "I'd like to get a little bit more consistency. Every time we go out we want to deliver really good performances. We're close to that stage. It doesn't help when you have to change personnel too often in the band because it can take pipers a year to get into the groove of how we play, how we approach the expression and phrasing of our MSRs and the type of music we will play in medleys. I wouldn't be suggesting that we're not playing up to standard because we have new people in the band, but I still feel that our consistency is not as good as I would like it to be at this stage, but it's close."

Terry is working hard with the current members of the band to get from 'it's close' to 'we're there'. "I would always prefer to have pipers who are capable of playing in Grade 1, but obviously they have to be able to bring something to the party. When the time comes that they're taking from the party then that's when you need to draw the line. A good average player is one that would be at band practice twice a week, will do exactly as he is asked, and who will focus on his instrument. I'm not going to say I would like to have a band full of them because that's not going to work either. You do need quality players, and we have many really good quality players, but we've also got some above average players who, to be honest, might struggle in another Grade 1 band unless they were in a position where they could be at practice two or three times a week. As long as they're still bringing something to the party that will be fine. At the end of the day, pipers who are coming to practice on a regular basis will play very well together, they will be very confident about playing with others around them as long as their instrument is operating one hundred percent and they can blow it one hundred percent. You've got to be able to blow the sound and we've got great people like that, some of the finest players in the country. That makes us a good strong unit."

While Terry reckons it's always nice to have some really great players in the band, they can bring problems. "We've had great players in the past, and what I find about some of them is that they have a tendency to do their own thing. They have a tendency to believe that what they are doing is one hundred percent correct. You can manage the average player and tell them, for example, to hold that note a little bit longer and they'll do it, whereas some of the greater players may think that they are already doing it. That can be difficult to deal with but I am very fortunate that over many years as pipe major I have noticed that I command respect for my opinion. The great players we have in our band today understand now that it has to be one person's opinion, whether he's right or wrong. If everyone is doing it exactly the same way then that's what will win prizes at the end of the day. The pipe corps will be playing perfectly in unison. Some of the better pipers in the band, and there are some now whose age and experience means they will be playing better than I would be, do have the respect for one who has been there for so many years. They have respect for the way I want to do things. They just do it."

Although Terry doesn't believe that the pipe major has to be the best player in the band, it can help. "You do have to be able to stand up and demonstrate to people how it is that you want things done and not just talk about it. You have to be able to show people how to do it and in that regard it makes me work harder at home because I'm competing against young players who are very good. They have respect and they know the way we approach music, especially with our MSRs. They know the amount of work we put into playing with good expression and in unison and with good phrasing. During the winter months we focus a lot on our technique and making sure that everyone plays the same way as each other. So there's a lot of work goes on and as far as I'm concerned it's great that the younger players are getting an education from it as well."

Terry works very hard on the standard of his own playing to help motivate the rest of the band, but sometimes it doesn't work and he has to deal with a player who isn't pulling his or her weight. "There have been times that I have been disillusioned. It always seems a little bit sad when you have the majority of your group that are working really hard and a small minority of the group that will always put things on the long finger and wait until closer to the time before they start working. That can be frustrating for pipers and drummers to put up with. In the real world, if they're not up to speed they wouldn't play, but it's always better to keep plenty of players there whether they are pipers or drummers."

One of Terry's main jobs as pipe major is to ensure that motivation is high, and it's not always easy. "It can be difficult to motivate people but one of the best ways I've found to do that is to update the material every year. We would try to learn a new MSR ever year, or change the structure of the tunes in the medley. Generally, every year we would learn a new medley or maybe half of a medley and that in its own way is good motivation for people because if you continue to play the same music as you played last year and the year previous then there is no incentive for people to take out their practice chanter, or to take out their pipes, or, for that matter, even to come to band practice. I think there is good motivation and good incentive if the material is changed on a regular basis and that's what we've done all along. Another good incentive is concert. Our band had done many concerts over the last ten years. They usually take place in March, and that is a great incentive for the lads to buckle down in the winter months and learn new material at a time of year when they wouldn't normally bother."

Practice is important to Terry Tully, not least because he reckons that the standard of playing in Grade 1 in particular is as high as it has ever been, and this is likely to make winning the major competitions more and more difficult as time goes on. "Over the years in Grade 1 the standard of the bands has risen. If you compare the standard of a winning performance in Grade 1 today to that of twenty-five years ago, the difference is incredible."

There are several reasons for that. "An awful lot of that has to do with education. I've seen it because I've lived it. People like John Wilson and Jim Wark came over here twenty-five years ago to educate us and pass on their knowledge to me, and others like me, and without them I certainly wouldn't know as much as I know. I think generally what has taken place is that the sound of the instrument has improved over the years. There are better quality chanters and better reeds. People who are setting the sound know exactly what they are looking for and are probably much more selective in what they are choosing for their chanters. There's a vast amount of information around to help people with how long you'll get from your instrument before it starts to give you trouble and what's causing the trouble, and this has played a major role in improving bands. I think that anyone would agree that the sound that some Grade 3 and Grade 2 bands can produce today is far superior to what any of the Grade 1 bands were producing twenty-five to thirty years ago. The performance that Grade 1 bands were winning with twenty-five years ago would probably only win Grade 3 today. That's all down to better quality products, better education, and more people knowing exactly how the instrument is working."

Outwith the competition arena, SLOT has a fierce reputation as a concert band and Terry obviously enjoys this side of the band's year. "It's a different type of music that we play in concert. Obviously we include our MSR and medley intact, but after that we create a nice musical effect with the use of other musical instruments such as keyboards, banjo, guitar and flutes. We've used lots of different instruments for our concert material and we would also try to mix the traditions in terms of the music we play."

"We would play Spanish and Breton music as well as traditional Irish, traditional Scottish, and modern contemporary music. I think it's very important because pipe bands have to move forward and anyone going to a concert who expects to hear a pipe band playing from the beginning to the end is living in the past. You can't do that. If you want to try to educate the general public then you have to mix other instruments with pipes and drums. Let people see how versatile the instrument can be."

There is no question that Terry Tully has allowed the world to see the versatility of the bagpipe in the years that he has been in charge of the St Laurence O'Toole Pipe Band. The time will come when he won't be in charge but he reckons that there will still be a Tully at the helm. "My father took over the role in 1964 so from then until the present day it has been led by a Tully. It's almost half the life of the band so I would like to think that my son Alen would be the next pipe major of the band, and I'm sure he will be. As to how long he will continue as pipe major nobody knows. I don't think anyone taking over today will be able to go through the same hardship that I went through and keep at it."

Terry might then be able to spend a bit more time with his family. The family that has allowed him to take the band where he has over the last forty years, and without whose support he would have struggled. "It can get very tiring when things are left to the pipe major all the time. I have to do a lot of work at home and have to make decisions that are not always popular. There is also a huge amount of work that goes on in the background and it would be the same for any pipe major in any band. People don't always realise it. If it wasn't for the support of family then I wouldn't be able to do it. I have a very supportive wife who will sit and watch TV on her own because she knows that I have to get chanters ready for the next practice or that I have to have music ready to send out by email. She doesn't really mind because she knows it is for a good cause."

Like so many others in these pages, it's all done without thought of payment for services rendered. "For the last three years I have been officially unemployed because of the recession in Ireland. I make a few shillings selling merchandise and I do a bit of teaching. I travel abroad to teach and I'm surviving without a problem. I'm fortunate in that I don't owe anyone any money and so I don't need an awful lot to survive. So that frees up my time to do a lot of work for the band. I suppose I'm a full-time pipe major for the SLOT."

Gordon Walker

Gordon Walker was four years old when he decided he wanted to be a piper. Two of his uncles, Jim and Bert, were pipers in the Scots Guards and as soon as his grandmother showed him pictures of them in their uniforms playing, he was hooked. "I told my folks that I wanted to be a piper and they took me to Pipe Major David Kay, a family friend, from my home town of Cumnock. I was four and a half when I had my first lesson and because I didn't know the relationship between the alphabet and music I had to learn by ear and by copying David's fingers. We had a weekly lesson at his house."

In common with many of the pipers in these pages, a close bond developed between teacher and pupil, but more than that in this case since Gordon became almost an adopted member of David's family. "David Kay became my 'uncle' and his wife Jean my 'auntie' because I went there every week until I joined the Army when I was sixteen. Then, even when I came home from the Army on leave, I would go and visit him and run through my tunes before I went to play at a competition. He was a great help and a great influence. He had taught teams and teams of pipers before me and they were all good players. His son, also David, was a piper with Shotts and Dykehead, and his son-in-law Hugh was a drummer with them as well."

An introduction to the Army sealed Gordon's fate as far as his early career was concerned. "We used to go to the caravan site in Inverness in the summer and the Royal British Legion played in the islands across from the park. The late Willie MacDonald was the Pipe Major and of course I'd heard of the band and that had an influence. The Royal Highland Fusiliers (RHF) recruitment team used to visit Cumnock and I became friendly with them. They used to take me up to their piping weekends at Bridge of Don and I got an introduction to the Army that way. It was great and I got the chance to see what barrack life was all about. I went to their piping school and found out what I would be doing if I joined up."

Join up he did, on the 10th January 1984, at the tender age of sixteen. He spent his first two years in the Army in Aberdeen before being moved to Berlin to join the Regiment, where he played under Pipe Major Gavin Stoddart. At twenty he was selected for sit the Pipe Major's course at Edinburgh Castle. "It was quite young but you should remember that Captain John MacLellan was appointed Pipe Major at nineteen. I think that it's not so much your age, it's your ability."

It's clear that Gordon had the ability. He won his first piping competition at the age of ten, playing 'Leaving Glen Urquhart', and by the age of sixteen had a Silver Medal under his belt as well. His competing career flourished while he was a soldier, thanks in part to great support from his Regiment. "Our ability to compete while I was in the army was dependent on where we were posted but the RHF was good to both me and Gavin Stoddart. They made sure that we were sent back as much as we could. We sometimes got attached to HQ in Glasgow and would go around with their recruiting team in the caravan and get round the Highland games. It was good PR for the Army of course that the likes of Gavin and I were winning prizes. I owe a lot to the regiment for giving me the chance to compete."

Gordon's life in the Army wasn't all pipes and drums. "You had to adapt to whatever your battalion was doing at the time, even if you were a piper. In Edinburgh at the Castle you would have to do the usual guard duties, and likewise when we went up to Balmoral. You weren't piping all the time, you had to be part of battalion life, but when you got the chance you made the most of it. Playing at the Officers' Mess, for example, was always good fun and we got out with the Pipes and Drums at the weekend. You would have to get the combats on, the kilts off, and put the pipes under the bed while we went to the prairies of Canada, or Kenya, for eight weeks at a time. We took the pipes with us when we went away. We even took them to the Gulf War with us but I don't know whether it was the sand, the air, or the different temperature, but the silver tarnished quite a bit and we had to leave them in the four tonne trucks. I had taken my good Lawrie pipes, and if I had thought more I would have had an Army set fitted up for that. I took them anyway and we had the odd chance to play when things cooled down a bit. We managed to practice and did a few local gigs. I was always in B Company and there were maybe about eight of us attached to Pipes and Drums who would get together to play for PR events."

During Gordon's pipe major's course he was taught how to teach, as well as the man management of a pipe band, and the history of the famous pipers of the past. "The course was great. Being a piper in the army gave me the sense of seeing the great players that had come before me and the funny thing I discovered was that nearly all of them were Corporals when they won their first Gold Medals — Corporal Willie Ross, Corporal GS McLennan, Corporal Donald MacLeod, and then in modern times Corporal Alistair Gillies, and then me. Also, for eight months, while I was on my course at the Castle, I got to sleep above the Crown Jewels every night."

After fifteen years in the Army, and with the rank of Sergeant, Gordon Walker decided the time was right for a change in career. "I spent my last six months in HQ in Glasgow doing a bit of teaching, and when I came out I had my first three months teaching with Robert Wallace at the College of Piping in Glasgow. I really enjoyed that, and then a job came up at the National Piping Centre. It was full-time with a salary so was more stable. I was there for five years and in the last year the school I am currently teaching in asked me to go out and do some supply work. Eventually the post came up full-time and I applied for it and got it, and I've now been there nine or ten years."

It's been nine or ten good years for Gordon. "I now teach in one school, St Columba's in Kilmacolm, although the work is split between the junior and the senior school. I'm at the junior school Monday, Tuesday and the senior school the rest of the week. I've got forty-six pupils at the moment and the school band plays at a lot of fixtures for the school, as well as some competitions. We went to Tartan Day in New York in April, and we've just got a new set of drums so the band is in a really healthy position at the moment."

While piping is an important part of his students' timetable, Gordon knows there are other demands on their time as well, and he sees his role as wider than just the day-to-day lessons he gives. "The band competes in school competitions but it's difficult because there are so many other commitments; sports and the Duke of Edinburgh awards and the like, but they do compete when they can. My job is to make sure that I give them as much as I can in the way of teaching and to introduce them to piping and the pipe band world in the hope that they will carry it on."

Gordon spends his days teaching and his evening playing, with pipe bands and a hugely successful solo competing and recital schedule. When he left the Army he played with Scottish Power Pipe Band until one day he received a visit from an old Army colleague. "I got a visit from Captain Hunter of the 52nd Lowland Regiment based in Maryhill. Their Pipes and Drums were struggling a bit and they were looking to recruit, and he came round to see if he could sway me back into uniform. He came up to the Pipers Tryst at the Piping Centre for a coffee and a chat and asked me if I would go to see the Colonel of the Regiment, Colonel Pickard, who I knew anyway. They showed me the Pipes and Drums Hall and it was great. When I asked if I could meet the rest of the band I was told that therein lies the difficulty, there was only one piper left! Corporal John Ferguson. They wanted me to recruit a band, including a leading drummer."

A huge task, but he did it, and they were ready to go in Grade 2 by the start of the next season with 15 pipers. So how did he manage it? "Lots of lies! It was a new band going into Grade 2 with new uniforms so they would look good and of course the TA paid for all the buses to take us wherever we were going, gave us food and they paid us to play, with double wages for the weekend and quarter or half wages when we practiced, so the guys were getting paid as well. We got into Grade 2 because they knew the calibre of the pipers — Finlay Johnston, Tam Campbell, Gary Caruthers, Calum MacCrimmon, and lots of students who would come in and out for a season or two. We lasted five years and did really well. I am pleased and proud to say that we were the best in the army, lifting thirty-two trophies in one year alone."

As so often happens with pipe bands though, the members found it difficult to maintain the momentum of combining military duties with band work, even although the conditions were better than in many civilian bands. "The TA band ran on the same basis as a regular unit, smart band with lots of uniforms, but it was difficult to retain the band because the army wanted them to be soldiers and I told the Colonel that the guys were there as musicians. They were all professional men in their own right, many of them married with families, who were only really there for the piping. I told him they would vote with their feet, that there would be nobody left, and that's what happened. We got down to eight or nine pipers and I asked the guys if they wanted to split up and go their own way to other bands but they all said no. They would rather stick with me. We would go as a unit to Civvy Street."

So Gordon's pipe band story moved on to the next stage. "The Mauchline and District Pipe Band had been defunct for eight years or so but they did still have some gear left so we went there, and we're still there. We're looking for sponsorship but it's not easy these days. We're competing in Grade 2, and in fact a couple of years ago we came first equal with Inveraray and District Pipe Band in piping at the World's and third overall. That's our claim to fame with Mauchline. The trouble is that when you get someone who is really good the Grade 1 bands want to rope them in. You bring them up to the standard you want and then the Grade 1 bands come along and lure them away. It's a hard one to deal with; you just have to try your best to provide good music. Sponsorship helps, and it's always good to be able to provide the guys with trips from time to time. We haven't been very lucky with that recently."

All of this work with pipe bands would be enough to keep most people busy, but not Gordon Walker. He is widely recognised as one of the most successful, and most entertaining, solo pipers of his generation and he has a very full recital schedule as well. He loves everything about the music and manages his life to suit. "It's not easy. Sometimes if there is a band practice twice a week you need to grab something to eat, whether it's fish and chips or something to sit-in, then you go to band practice. You're maybe not getting home until eleven at night. I'm on my own so I need to fit in housework; washing and cooking and stuff. I get there but it just takes me a bit longer I suppose. It's difficult finding a balance. I live a busy and hectic solo life with concerts and recitals and the like but you just have to plough through the busy times until it slackens a bit."

Gordon has certainly ploughed through some busy times since that first competition win at the age of ten and he has very fond memories of all of the successes he has enjoyed over the years. "The Silver Medal that I won at sixteen at Oban stands clear in my mind. It was a great day and the family was with me. It was quite a hard thing in those days as you had to play twice. There was an A and a B group and the top six from each group went into a final of twelve. It was held on the main stage in the Corran Hall and I came out trumps that day so that stands out there as one of the best. My Gold Medals, one for Oban and one for Inverness, are milestones and still stand out for me. It's the important ones that you remember, the Gold Medals, the Silver Chanter and The Glenfiddich. I loved the feeling when I won the Silver Chanter and I liked playing that day. I also liked winning the Lord Todd. It's a bit different, more like a recital than a competition, and the audience really enjoys these types of event. There is a bar there and there are groups of folk having a drink and shouting at you. You know your music has been well-received when you get that sort of response."

Gordon Walker is a consummate professional and his preparation for events, whether concert, recital or competition, is meticulous. "Preparation is vital. The Glenfiddich Competition is a good example, where they want six tunes in each category. You have a mental list, and I have one that I keep in my case as well. Every time I'm getting ready for a competition or recital I'm not just having a practice but I also visualise myself on stage. When I go through to my piping room in the house I have the settee where the judges' bench would be and the audience would be at the opposite end, so when I'm playing my march I'm careful not to ever turn my back on any judge if I can avoid it. If I'm marching I would turn in toward the judges one way and then turn the other so you're really doing a big figure of eight. I'm mentally preparing myself and if I can get a couple of hours hard practice in a day then that's fine. Then the next day I'll alternate the tunes."

Gordon reckons that you can't get straight into your routine of preparing as a competition piper when the pipes are cold so he'll play some 6/8 marches and then, when he thinks the pipes are warmed up, and he is too, he'll start his session proper with some light music. Three sets of MSR, then a pìobaireachd in one session, and then have a rest. If he's up for it, and if he has enough time, he'll do it all again. He alternates the tunes every day so that he can run through them all, checking on the instrument as he goes.

Things don't always go to plan on the day, no matter how much you prepare. "I was about twenty-three when I won my first Gold Medal at Oban and I played the 'Prince's Salute'. The pipes had been great all season up to the morning of Oban but when I took them out the box to tune them up all of the drones stopped and I thought 'What's going on here?'. They were cane reeds in those days and you had to blow down them to get them started. I got them going and then I went to empty the water trap. When I was taking the trap out the actual stock was turning so I thought 'What else could possibly go wrong here?'"

Even with all of that going on, Gordon still managed to perform to the judges' satisfaction. "It went fine. The judges were Ronnie Lawrie, Donald MacPherson and Captain Andrew Pitkeathly. I had been going to Andrew for lessons, and he said to the other judges that this was one of his pupils and that he would have to sit it out. He said that if there had been strange results then he would have intervened but there was no question, he said, that I had done enough to win the Gold Medal that day. I thought I had done enough to win. I was really pleased with the performance. The pipes were lovely. When you get the pipes locked in in any competition it's great. As soon as they go out of tune you've got a fight on your hands, so I was pleased with the way they sounded, especially given what had happened earlier in the day. It was the same at Inverness when I won the Gold Medal. I played 'MacKay's Banner' and the pipes were going like bells."

So the day that started really badly came good in the end. On other days, however, when you think you've done enough to win some sort of prize, you can come away with nothing. "Donald MacLeod used to talk to his pupils about the days you come off the platform thinking you've played badly yet you win a prize. He said that there is a balance, because on some days you'd go to a competition and your pipes, or even you, are not in the groove and you think that it could have been better but the results come out and you've won. You take the prize and say thanks. At other times you go to a competition and think you've done really well and you don't get a mention. You go away and fight another day. I suppose there are days where you wonder where the judges are coming from and how they decided on the prizes, but it doesn't happen very much. Judges have their reputation to think about as well and there will be someone making a comment to the organisers if we get strange results. It's a pretty honest game in the solo world; it's got to be. There are too many reputations at stake."

Gordon Walker's reputation is right up there, and has been for twenty-five years, so how does he keep it going now that he's in his mid-forties? "It's what I've always known, I'm part of the fraternity and it connects me with the great names of the past. The oldest man I saw competing was Evan MacRae when he won his Gold Medal at Oban well into his sixties. Then you hear things like John Macdonald of Inverness who was sixty-five when he won his last Clasp. I don't think I'll be competing at that age. In competition I'll play as long as I think I'm fit and I'm getting something good out of it. At that level the older you are the harder it gets. If it's evenly spread out and I'm doing a good job then I'll continue. There are names that have been at the top for twenty-five years. Willie McCallum, Roddy MacLeod, there was Alistair Gillies. Latterly Stuart Liddell has taken Alasdair's position, but you've got Jack Lee, Bruce Gandy, Chris Armstrong and Dougie and Jimmy Murray that could come in and do something. It's harder for Jack and Bruce being overseas and maybe not getting over here as much as they would like."

Gordon is well-known, and much loved, for his informal and entertaining style when playing at recitals, but he would like to see some changes made to the way these events are organised. "The audience can be tense and I'd like them to be a bit more relaxed. Perhaps the organisers could do something to seat the audience at tables and chairs and have a bar open to let them relax and have a nice time. It's not meant to be a competition."

It's an interesting view, and one not shared by a lot of his colleagues who enjoy the formality of recital, and see no difference between treading the boards at a major competition and giving a recital. Although Gordon likes the event to be more relaxed, he approaches the evening with the same level of preparation. "With this world we live in there could be people sitting in the audience recording what you're playing with hand-held devices, even filming, and the next thing somebody tells you they've seen you on YouTube when it had nothing to do with you, and you might not even have seen it. That could be embarrassing at times but I don't know if anything can be done about that to make it above board. You have to be aware that you're always potentially on camera."

"It used to be the case that recitals were a bit more relaxed and you could interact with the audience; talk with them and tell them a bit about the tunes. You can't do that in competitions. If you make a mistake in a recital it's not the end of the world, apart from the fact that the world could get to hear it. I do try to make the recital programme varied and as exciting as I can and cover all genres of the music. I like to give the audience as much of me as I possibly can, and make it relaxed for them. I don't like to see an audience sitting there tense because I've dropped a gracenote. So what, it's just a recital? People can put too much pressure on recitals. I don't see recitals being more stressful. It's an honour to be invited to do it and it's a chance to keep your name out there. People can hear it and say 'he's on form' and that's great as you head into the competition time."

Gordon likes to relax, not away from piping it has to be said, but by composing new tunes and he's very proud of the honour he had when he was asked to compose a special tune for a special birthday. "I wrote a tune for the Queen's Diamond Jubilee and played it in front of her at Braemar. I have the photos to prove it, and she thoroughly enjoyed it. She said that it must have been difficult coming up with something as original as that but once you get the basic melody in your head the rest of it comes along. I was delighted with the whole thing and the original is now sitting in Balmoral Castle."

Composition doesn't always come easy. "Sometimes you have to work hard at the ideas when you are writing. If you have to work hard then you're not in the right frame of mind and I'd put it down and go and do something else. But if you know that you need to do it, and if you keep your chanter and music book handy, you can get it written down or recorded as soon as something comes to you. Similarly with your phone, you can record on that nowadays. That small phrase could be the next tune, that wee question and answer phrase is where the shape of the tune could come from."

He is keen to continue writing but is also adamant that what he writes needs to meet the high standards of the tunes that are already out there. "Your standard tunes, 'Clan MacColl', 'Highland Wedding', and 'Argyllshire Gathering' are your standards and in forty years' time I think it will still be these standards that are played at the major competitions."

For all the prizes, recitals and honours that grace Gordon Walker's glittering career, he still likes nothing more than coming home back to play. "I do like my Burns Suppers in Ayrshire. I've piped in the haggis, addressed it and then piped it back out again. It's all about what you put into it. If you just stand about in the rain you'll get bored."

The most important part of what you have to put into it is practice. "When I was a wee boy my link to the outside piping world was the radio. Now there is so much with the internet and everything. I'd listen to people on the radio and think, how do they do that with ten fingers. I've got ten fingers and I can't do that. That would make me want to practice all the more. My mother always said that when I came in from school that the bag was dropped and it was away to my chanter or pipes, then I'd have a break when I got shouted for dinner, then it was back to it again and I just hammered the practice. Record yourself, that's a great way to prepare for competition. Record it and then listen, but don't listen straight away. Go and have a cup of tea first then come back with a pen and paper and listen and make notes. 'That tempo was a bit fast' or 'I need to change the expression in this bit.' Be your own judge, get the most out of it and practice all you can. It's common sense. If you put the practice in, you will gain the rewards later. The world's your oyster, the sky's the limit, and my advice to all young pipers is simply 'Go for it'."

Robert Wallace

Robert Wallace reckons that having a father who played jazz really helped his understanding of music in general, and the pipes in particular. "I didn't have a narrow view of music because my old man was a jazz musician. My early upbringing was all Gary Burton and the Modern Jazz Quartet, Lionel Hampton, Bud Powell and Miles Davies. I knew more about them than I did about Patrick Òg MacCrimmon, in fact I knew bugger all about him. The jazz was what I was brought up with through listening to my dad's music."

There was a strong musical connection in the Wallace household, but no connection with the bagpipes. In common with many in the West of Scotland when Robert Wallace was growing up, he had his early lessons in the Boys' Brigade. "We were playing football and had to stop because one of the guys said he had to go, 'Where are you going?' we asked. 'Chanter lessons, do you want to come too?'"

Robert Wallace wasn't a willing student initially, and it was the 'extras' that made him go back. "It was during the summer holidays, and at the time I didn't want to go, but my mum forced me to go and see old Alex who used to take in all the urchins in from the street and teach them. He used to give us all a big glass of orange juice and that was you in. His sister sent him maple syrup from Canada and he used to throw that down your neck as well. We went back, not so much for the piping, but for the maple syrup and orange juice. That was his psychology and lucky for me he was a very good teacher, a very strict teacher, and a stickler for technique. I was with him for a year learning the scale, and then it was into the band where I got my first tune, 'Loch Rannnoch', and a half set of pipes. None of us had any money for pipes. The idea of us having our own chanter or our own set of pipes was a joke, but luckily the Boys' Brigade had stuff that boys who were leaving at seventeen handed back and they got recycled to the new intake."

As well as the chanter and pipes being free, the other thing that was helpful for Robert Wallace when he started playing was the fact that the lessons themselves were also free. "People pay for lessons now, and in some ways that's good. I still think of piping as a folk art and one of the things that's great about that is there are men and women out there who are prepared to do it without

162

being paid. At the College of Piping we still do it as a charity if we have to. We still teach pupils who can't afford to pay because that is enshrined in our rules. If you think back to when the College was set up in the forties, not a lot of people in Glasgow had a lot of money, it's not a well-to-do city even today, but back then lots of people didn't even have an inside toilet. We did, but we had no running hot water, and we had to go to the baths. It all sounds very sad and deprived, but the baths were across the road. It was 4d to get in and that's how we got a wash. Otherwise we'd have to use kettles in the house. That's the way it was."

"People like Alex McIvor who taught the Boys' Brigade band and Alex Ibell who taught the wee boys, they were aware of all that. They would never have considered taking money from us. That was the first thing my mother asked that first night 'How much is it?', and when I told her he didn't take anything there was a sigh of relief. I suspect if he charged I wouldn't have been able to go back"

With a bit of lateral thinking the teachers were able to save Robert and his fellow students a bit more money, at the same time as encouraging them to read and write music. "There was one copy of Logan's Tutor which got handed round all of the boys, and when you had copied the whole book into your manuscript book then you passed it on. There were two reasons for it — one, it gave you your own tutor book because 4d for the manuscript was a lot less than the cost of the book itself, and two, because you had to write it out you maybe thought about it a bit more and learned a bit more as you were doing it, although when we came to some of the Italian music phrases at the end of the book it all became a bit of gobbledygook to a nine-year-old."

The same wouldn't happen today, partly because there is more money around, and partly because 'value' is judged differently according to Robert Wallace. "I don't think the teaching is any different or better because people are paying for it, and I think that dedicated teachers who are good at it will draw students to them. The difference is in the parents' attitude. There's so much money about today. Although Glasgow is a poor city, there is a lot of money around, relatively speaking, and you sometimes find that parents judge what they get by how much they pay. Wee Johnny comes here to learn to play the pipes, and I tell them it's going to be £30 an hour, then they go up to the Piping Centre and they say it's going to be £40 an hour, and where do they go? They go to the Piping Centre because it's more expensive and Johnny is their only son. That's just human nature. It doesn't make the teaching any better. I'm sure the Piping Centre does the same great job that we do."

It works the other way as well sometimes. "If you're too cheap people don't value it so you get some not turning up for lessons and they don't respect you as much as they would have done if they had to pay more for it. It's all about horses for courses and it's to do with character and personality, how mannerly people are, and their ability to assess things. You might give a kid a lesson for nothing in here and then you find that you'd be better charging him because he thinks it's a load of crap otherwise."

Then you might have children and parents with a different set of objectives. "The parents want their kid to be a champion but the kid might not want to be a champion. He might be happy learning 'Scots Wha Hae' or 'Amazing Grace'. It's all about what the student wants to achieve. You can tell them that they'll never be a solo piper, or never achieve Grade 1, but they can still enjoy their piping if they just set their level to what God's given them, which might be a pretty manky set of mitts. If they spend some time cleaning them up and learning to blow then they could get a lot of pleasure playing in a Grade 3 or Grade 4 band. You need to be honest with them, that's the approach, rather than telling them they can't do it."

There was no question that Robert Wallace was going to be able to do it, and the Boys' Brigade soon had him competing regularly. "As soon as I could play a set of pipes we would get a loan set, Joe Kidd would set them up for us, and off we'd go. You'll get some teachers who won't put their kids forward because they don't want the parents seeing a bad judge's sheet in case it reflects badly on the teacher. That didn't happen in the Boys' Brigade where we were always pushed into competition."

Success came quickly but so did a move from solo competition to the world of the pipe band. "I was reasonably successful at that, but at age eighteen I was a band guy. I had joined Muirhead & Sons after the Boys' Brigade. We were taught so well that the Grade 1 bands were always looking for pipers from Boys' Brigade bands. I had a lot to learn, principally about blowing. As far as the playing went it was fine, we wouldn't have been taken on otherwise because it was a very tough environment. The band went downhill when I joined them but up to that point they were a great playing band, absolutely wonderful, and in Bob Hardie you had a real maestro, a real musician."

Once he had settled into the way of things with Muirhead & Sons, and with a bit of help from Bob Hardie, Robert Wallace eventually got back into the solo groove. "We used to do an annual gig in Newtonmore at the games up there and we would come on and play a bit. Some of us decided to have a bash at the solos. I hadn't played in a solo competition since the boys' contests and I think I got second in the march in an open competition. The people in the band that heard me playing encouraged me to do more. I decided I would. It was difficult combining the solo with the band work, particularly with the pipes. Remember it was all sheepskin bags and cane reeds and it was a constant battle, not like it is nowadays. I hardly play that instrument now, but I can pick it up and within a day it's going. I couldn't have done that before. The bag would have needed to be re-tied or the valve would be sticking. Anyway, I got back into it in 1976 and had a bit of success. I did all right at Oban and I had started to play some pìobaireachd with Bob."

When Muirhead & Sons folded in 1979, Robert Wallace decided that the time was right to concentrate on his solo playing. "Bands are fantastic, and a great achievement, but unless you're a pipe major you end up being known as the guy that played with Muirhead's or the guy that played with Glasgow Police, you're not known as Robert Wallace. You might get a 'Did you win the Worlds with the Police?', but you're still just one of the band. It's like playing with Rangers when they won the cup. It's maybe a bit of ego, but I always felt that if you could be successful at it then why go into denial? Why not try to fulfil the ability you have been given, because a lot of people don't have that?"

Robert Wallace has a hugely successful competing career, and at the time was the one of the only pipers who managed to combine that world with the world of a piper playing in a folk band. It wasn't always easy. "I always made the point that I would never compromise the solos. If I was going to play in a folk band I was also was going to keep the solos going because I wasn't having people saying to me that I was only a ceilidh piper. It was very important then. I don't think it's quite as important now though. You can be a good respected piper, play in the folk scene, and not necessarily compete. Then it was very important for your self-respect to show that you could do both. I think that another thing about it was that doing the solo piping inculcated a certain discipline in your playing. If you were only playing folk stuff I think you would get lazy. As long as you're hitting B flat, don't worry about the gracenotes. That's great now that we're a bit older and can't quite get the fingers moving the same, but back then you had no hiding place."

Robert Wallace was keen to maintain his solo standards with the Whistlebinkies, but the non-pipers in the band had standards too. "I wanted to play well with the group and didn't want to cut any of the work out, and the solos were a better discipline for technique and for rhythm. With the folk band, with the bodhran going, you're driven along with everyone else and you don't have that rhythmical discipline that you have to have in solo piping to work out your own tempo and your own phrasing. It was hard. I just got them all to play like me. I used to say that if they wanted to play 2/4 marches we would play them, but we'd play them as pipe tunes. We'd play them the way they should have been played. If it was an Irish or a Shetland reel then I would have to change. That was the compromise, but we could do it because we were all good players."

It wasn't just the tunes that were the subject of compromise. "We had to think about the scales as well. Eddie McGuire could finger in B flat which was good for me, and for me that was the best key for the Lowland pipes. I didn't want to go down to A like a European bagpipe because it gets awful dull and flat; B flat is a much better key. It's got a great projection and it really sounds Scottish. The rest of the guys could play along in B flat, not so easy for the fiddle, but they all did it when they needed. Latterly, Mark has had a fiddle that he keeps tuned up. The flute and clarsach are no problem, but Stuart had some issues with his concertina and I think he changed some of the buttons. We were all prepared to make these compromises because we knew it would sound pretty good. Other instrumentalists used to think that three chords fitted any pipe tune, they had no idea of the scale that we played. It was hellish."

Not anymore. "Today there are some real high class and quality arrangements for the pipes, with people really thinking it through. It's moved on fantastically well. In the last forty years the pipes have become fully integrated into the Scottish tradition whereas before, when we started, it was a separate branch and ne'er the twain shall meet, so to speak."

The Whistlebinkies, or the Whisky-binkies as they were known in East Germany after a particularly raucous Festival there in the late seventies, grappled with some serious musical issues over the years. They also had a lot of fun. "Musically speaking, some of the best nights of my life have been when playing with the Whistlebinkies in terms of taking our music to another level and in understanding other musicians, not only other pipers and drummers."

This all came about thanks to a sore finger. "Jimmy Anderson was playing with the Clutha at the time. He was a joiner and he kept hurting his fingers and I used to have to stand in for him. That's literally what happened. He'd end up with these bloodied and bandaged hands and he'd ask me to play at one of these festivals.

The Whistlebinkies were there with Gordon Hotchkiss, Jim Daly and Big Mick Broderick. They were always seen as the poor man's Clutha. Gordon, like Jimmy, was from Falkirk and he did some of the old bothy songs, but the Whistlebinkies were much more Irish orientated with Big Mick giving it 'The Alamo' and all that stuff, Jim with his Irish fiddle tunes, and Eddie with his flute and classical stuff. They fancied having a piper and asked me and that's how it all started. Just being able to do gigs with Mick Broderick was amazing. It was all heavy bevvy and festivals and stuff but we were always quite serious musically as well."

The work that Robert Wallace started with the Whistlebinkies, and which so many others are continuing, has really helped widen the appeal of the Great Highland Bagpipe. "The idea that a folk group with pipes could fill an auditorium is great, although there have been certain commercial compromises that have had to be made. I've always gone on about the respectability that pipers received, and it's improved over the last ten years. It's slowly changing. We're not quite at the respect levels of the Bretons or the Asturians where you're a hero if you play the national instrument. We need to keep going the way we are. Suddenly we are getting noticed."

These days fewer of our youngsters have to rely on the Boys' Brigade for lessons. "Taking the pipes into colleges is great. The school at Plockton and the College of Piping, as well as the National Piping Centre, are all helping to make the changes. Then there are the bands as well. Lots of schools now have bands, and bands like George Watson and Boghall have huge programmes for kids. That has to be paying dividends."

None of this has happened overnight. "If you think back to when the schools got 'O levels' in 1974, from then on the increase in respect can be seen. That's the time it takes to alter the psyche of a nation and if you think back to what it was like in the sixties and seventies then there is a huge difference now."

As well as changes in the education system, there have been great political changes in Scotland since the seventies, but Robert Wallace is not sure whether the changes to the music helped the politics or vice versa. "Devolution has maybe played a part in it, but I think what was happening with our music was happening before the politics. Maybe the politics has come in on the back of the music."

Robert thinks that now that the Parliament is here, it needs to do more. "It's been a regret of mine that since the Parliament opened it has made not one bit of difference to the funding of piping. There is still no central fund, no means of the national music being directly supported the way orchestra, opera and ballet is. I'm not for a minute suggesting that these other forms of music shouldn't get support, just that we should get it as well. It's a political failing and it's a failing of government. Politicians need to say 'This is the national music and we need to support it'."

Robert believes that pipers should be seen as a special case. "The politicians need to understand that other traditional instrumentalists can find work that pipers can't. Most fiddlers, pianists and harpists can get commercial work in bars and clubs, work that pipers can't get on their own. They also need to understand that there is a huge contribution to the national wellbeing economically from piping. Look at the money that Piping Live! brings to the city, and The World Championships organised by The Royal Scottish Pipe Band Association. A huge amount of money. I would be surprised if a tenth of that gets back to the people supplying it."

It's crucial that more of this money comes back to the grass roots of piping according to Robert Wallace. "We need to keep making the right decisions. We need the politicians to start putting back some of the money that comes into piping. There shouldn't be a situation where a juvenile band can't get money to hire a bus to go to a competition. Bands up in Inverness should be able to come to Glasgow and the RSPBA should be given money to disburse to under-18 bands. They should be getting help and it shouldn't all be left to parents running jumble sales. It just needs the political will to do the same as is done for Scottish Opera. Someone needs to say to us 'here's your block grant'. It should go to a committee in charge of disbursing it, and the committee should be made up of those in a position to make the right decisions. If the bands are properly registered and send you their receipts then you pay the bills that allow them to travel to the events. There are ways of doing it. It would be simple, straightforward and easy to do."

Robert reckons this would be fairer than the way things operate at the moment. "The current situation where the Piping Centre gets a whole load of dough because they can pull the strings, and I'm not saying it's not used properly, causes ill feeling and it shouldn't be there. There is an easier way to do it. That's the next step I'd like to see. The institutions like the Piping Centre and College of Piping would get a pro rata slice of the cake from Central Government that would also free us up to raise our own money. Private income is fine, but it needs public money as well."

If the money is found to help the next generation of pipers then who knows where it could lead. "As Robert Mathieson says, 'Piping is a disease', and when you get a bit of success at something you want to do something with it. I used to say, when I was doing well at Oban and Inverness, that for a wee guy from Whiteinch with the arse hanging out my trousers, here I am sharing a tuning room with John D. Burgess and all these big names. Playing for Gold Medals and all that. I've played at the Vatican for the Pope. The doors that can be opened are amazing, but that's just music. If you can get into music then do it. Even if you do end up in a Grade 3 band, piping is no different. Last year one of the worst bands in the world got flown to China for the Winter Olympics just because somebody knew somebody. It does open doors and it is well worth the effort. At times it's a hell of an instrument, but then it's very rewarding in lots of other ways."

John Wilson

That John Wilson would end up playing the pipes was never in doubt. His father William was a piper in the 8th Battalion Argyll and Sutherland Highlanders. His uncle, pipe major of the 8th Battalion, was killed, like a lot of his colleagues, leading the Battalion into battle at Longstop Hill in 1942. The battalion suffered heavy casualties in what was one of the decisive engagements in the North Africa campaign, and the Wilson family, and the piping scene in general, lost a gifted and talented player.

After the war John's father became pipe major of the Campbeltown and District Pipe Band and the young Wilson found himself drawn to the music. "It started for me with a house that was always full of young pipers all being taught by my father, and as a toddler I was brought up in that environment. My father had a very small practice chanter made for me when I was four or five and I would sit in with the boys and try to imitate what was going on."

This informal involvement didn't last long and soon Wilson senior decided that his son should take his piping to the next level. "The serious stuff started when I was about six, that's when my father told me I needed to start to learn to play the chanter. He taught me in a very standard way in the sense that we went through the exercises and got together with the embellishments, the ornamentation, how to play those properly, and then he would show me one or two basic tunes in terms of understanding timing and rhythm."

After John had picked up his first couple of tunes the teaching regime changed, and Wilson senior surprised his son with the direction he took. "He taught me pìobaireachd! I always remember that he gave me 'Salute to Donald' and 'The Massacre of Glencoe'. I could play them both before I could play the 'Glendaruel Highlanders' and I was only six years old. He used to tell me that pìobaireachd was the ultimate challenge and that if you could handle the subtleties that were required, and you can handle the technical demands, then the rest would be simple."

It wasn't long before John was strutting his stuff on the competition boards, and from his first outing he has had a phenomenally successful competition career. "My father was the man who took me through the initial stages and through junior piping where I was very successful from a young age. I competed for the first time at Cowal when I was barely nine and got second in the marches."

After this early success, John's teaching was altered to include tuition from the great Donald MacLeod, but it is to his father that John remains grateful for that early work. "My father put in place the basic strands of maintaining my instrument, tuning it and building up the repertoire of MSR and pìobaireachd before I went to Donald MacLeod."

His early lessons with Donald involved what would nowadays be called 'distance learning' and it was actually a number of months after the start of their lessons that the two actually met. "I was about ten when I first went to Donald and we communicated initially through the medium of reel-to-reel tape. Donald would send me a tape with two pìobaireachds on it and I would return a tape with my version of the tunes. Donald would then return a tape to me with a critique on the tunes and another two to learn. And so it went on. Maybe six or eight weeks passed between Donald sending me the tunes and me receiving his feedback, so in a fairly short space of time I had built up a repertoire of eighteen or twenty tunes."

Eventually the teacher and pupil actually met. "In the early years I couldn't have told you what he looked like. He could have been a giant of six foot five inches like Ronnie Lawrie. I didn't pay attention to music books so had no idea. You can imagine the first time I met him in Glasgow for a lesson was a great surprise and thrill."

Although the best part of half a century has passed since these early lessons John Wilson remembers them fondly and talks enthusiastically about Donald Macleod's teaching style, love, and knowledge of the music. "I remember the first tape that I was sent contained 'Glengarry's March' and 'Lament for Patrick Òg MacCrimmon'. He told me they were both extremely challenging pieces. On the one hand you had the perception of 'Glengarry's March' as a small tune that didn't demand much when in reality the phrasing and expression demanded a great deal. Then you had the 'Lament for Patrick Òg' which was a classic and the technical difficulty and the phrasing challenges were there to be seen. The challenge in that tune was proving yourself able to handle it. I always remember him saying on the tapes, 'Here's a big tune that you need to be able to handle, and, by the way, here's a wee one that you may think is not that difficult but the difficulty is that the big focus has to be on phrasing and movement'. He wanted to get his message across because he was very much into forward movement in his phrasing and shading in his playing, and he wanted to give you early examples of that. His singing was just wonderful and that is the real way to communicate when you are teaching someone. I still use it all the time. It is the only way to get people to understand the nuances of style and expression because you can't demonstrate that just by playing or by looking at the staff notation."

John has a real passion for his music and it is obvious that he was deeply affected by the years he spent with Donald MacLeod. Having said that, he is also conscious of the way he introduces pìobaireachd to his students today. While he is keen to show his pupils the delights of pìobaireachd early on, he is also aware that for some it can be daunting. "I am very quick to get them on to pìobaireachd. You can sometimes see their wee faces when you mention it and you see the sudden realisation that I'm going to teach them 'that slow stuff'. Pìobaireachd is held in a sort of mystique and, while I don't wish to be disrespectful to the academics, it can be a feeding ground for them, something which can be off-putting for beginners who can only go on what they have heard about it. I firmly believe that it is the music of the people. It was there before the light music so it's even more a part of our musical heritage."

John has a reputation for being quick with an opinion if he believes strongly in something. It's obvious he believes in the importance of what we now call the 'classical music' within piping, although he would probably be upset with that label. "There is a bit of mystique about pìobaireachd that is misplaced and there is also a bit of snobbery attached to it. That's a difficult word to use for someone that was steeped in and brought up with pìobaireachd, and taught by canntaireachd, from the minute I put a chanter in my mouth. I got pìobaireachd from my father and from Donald MacLeod for twenty-odd years and so I'm not being disrespectful to them when I say that, but there is a wee bit of snobbery there and it irks me. Some purists get offended when players mess about with the theme of a pìobaireachd. Now, I'm not saying that we shouldn't respect it and hold it in esteem, but we should also be open minded with the music. Be grateful that people are recognising that not only is it a fundamental part of what the Great Highland Bagpipe is about but that it has value as music."

John left school and Campbeltown at the same time as his studies took him to Edinburgh. "I left in 1967 to go to Herriot Watt University to study architecture. When it came to my year out, after three years of studies, I decided that I didn't have the flair to be a really good architect. I had visited a few firms and had seen people in their fifties sitting doing development drawings (and I hope no architect out there in their fifties takes exception to this) and I thought that it didn't fit in with what I had joined up for. I became an architect to get the opportunity to be creative and get involved in design teams. It became clear that it was quite a strict drawn-out apprenticeship and a lot of people didn't achieve their aspirations."

For John Wilson, it wasn't just disillusionment with the course that made him leave university. "The piping was suffering terribly as well. I was still competing but I wasn't achieving what I thought I should be. I was going to competitions when I thought I was ill-prepared. The course was really tough and took a lot of time. Studio time took up day to day work and I was studying a lot at night so I wasn't getting a lot of piping in, and that played a big part in the decision."

It was easy for John to decide what route to take, but others in the same situation might find it more difficult. "Things worked out okay for me and it's easy for me to say that when you hit the crossroads you need to go where your heart tells you to go and things will be okay. You have to make that conscious decision. For me it was easier because I realised I had probably made the wrong decision in the first place. I was a people person and I had to look for a job that allowed me to use these skills."

That job and these skills took John to Glasgow and a hugely successful career in first Glasgow and, subsequently, Strathclyde Police ending up with the rank of Chief Superintendent and Divisional Commander of A Division in one of the force's highest profile jobs, in charge of policing Glasgow city centre. "When I left university I was looking for a job that would let me be out there dealing with people. In 1971 I joined the City of Glasgow Police. Although it was the career that attracted me I joined with the view that it might give me a bit more time for my own piping, but the pipe band wasn't at the forefront of my mind. I had a view from day one that if the Police Service turned out to be the right job I could make a good solid career out of it. I would have a good structured working pattern and would find time for practice and competition."

His move to the City of Glasgow Police did indeed allow him to devote more time to practice and this led to a hugely successful career in solo piping as well as great success with the Police Pipe Band. "I got right back into competition. I won the Senior Piobaireachd at Oban in 1971 and that was the start of my competing getting back on track. Then the band came into play. Angus MacDonald was the band president and Ronnie Lawrie had just stepped down as pipe major in favour of Ian McLellan and there was an approach asking me to join. I started playing in the band under Ian and from 1972 to 1974 we were on the rise. We had a lot of people coming in who were really good players.

Jim Wark joined the same day as me; David Pirie came from the Scots Guards, and Alistair Ross from the 214th Boys' Brigade. You sensed that something was on the boil. We won the World Championship in 1976 for the first time and that was the beginning of the ascendency."

It wasn't all plain sailing, however. "There were people like me and Gregor McLeod who were finding that there was a conflict between career development and playing in the band, and a number of players left. In 1979 some band members had a meeting with the then Chief Constable Patrick Hamill. He was told in no uncertain terms that there was a clear conflict between divisional management and their overview of people who played in the band, gauged against their potential to progress in the force. As a result of that meeting he formed the Strathclyde Police Pipe Band Band Unit. After that the issue of career development was removed from the division and passed centrally to HQ to avoid the perception that there was an element of prejudice in terms of career development because you were in the band."

As well as helping band members with the issue of career development the formation of the Band Unit acted as a platform for one of the most successful periods that any Pipe Band has enjoyed at any level of competition. "When the Band Unit was formed was when the band went from strength to strength and we went on the famous run from 1980 to 1986, and so it went on until I left the band at the tail end of 1989. Just after that, following another promotion, I effectively gave up solo competition as well when I realised that it was no longer viable in terms of giving it the time it needed."

By now John was well on the way to a successful career in the Police but he also continued with this interest in piping by moving from the competition board to the judge's seat. "It was a natural progression for me to move to judging, but I'm not suggesting it should be for everyone. There is an issue that competing pipers want to look at judging panels, look at the individuals, and feel confident in the profile of these individuals as people who have 'done it and got the t-shirt'. There are others who would argue that because you are a top class piper, or played in a top class band at the very top level, it doesn't naturally follow that you will be a good adjudicator. There is an element of truth in that, but I didn't find any conflict. I think being a policeman helps a lot as a judge. It's about clarity of thought and assimilation in how you rate one performance against the other twenty-eight or so that you have to listen to."

John Wilson believes that credibility in the eyes of the competitors can only come from success in the competition arena, but that there are exceptions to this rule. "I can reflect back on my early days and look at people like James Campbell of Kilberry and Archie Kenneth who were extremely well regarded authorities in piping but weren't successful senior pipers by any means. There were very few people who would have argued against their credibility and their place on senior judging benches. Their credibility came from their background in pìobaireachd. James Campbell was the son of Archibald Campbell of Kilberry who had drawn up the Kilberry Collection. I can remember that he once sat beside me in the audience during an MSR competition and admitted that light music was not his forte and that he related much more strongly to pìobaireachd. Now there are pipers out there who would say that you can't have somebody sitting on a judging bench who admits that they know a lot about pìobaireachd but they don't really relate to light music."

John reckons that the preparation and time that competitors give to their art these days means that they have to have confidence in the panel that is testing them. "It's such a serious business now. The pipers of today have a great sense of what it's all about. They know how much work they have put in to get to the levels they have reached and in stretching themselves. They have to feel that the people who are sitting in front of them totally understand what it's all about."

While he is adamant that competitors need to have respect for the judges he is also vocal on the lack of musicality that he hears in some performances. "I still feel that there has been a 'competition' frame of mind developing that is a bit unhealthy in terms of performing. People see the concert performance and the competition performance as two entirely different things and I think that the perceived message that has come out from judges has contributed to this as well. The individual aspect of interpretation seems to have been sterilised. Many pipers think that the whole ethos of playing in a competition is having a good set of pipes, not making any technical errors, and in terms of timing and general expression, just keeping it 'right down the middle'. I have judged competitions where I have sat and heard the same type of performance time after time after time. Good bagpipes, good solid fingering, but not a lot to excite you, not a lot to generate any sense of emotion. It is pipers being very careful and cautious and almost, to some extent, just going through the motions."

John has his own views on how this needs to change. "Change has to come from competitors and judges alike. I would love to see closer links between the Competing Pipers' Association and the adjudication panel. It would be great to see, for example, a composite workshop between those two groups sitting down and talking about performance and what it is all about. I don't wish my colleagues on the adjudication register to think for one minute I'm suggesting that they are totally responsible for this because they are not. I've spoken to competitors who have admitted that they look at judging panels and then they try to decide how to play. As a performer I never did that. I played what was in my soul. In terms of MSR playing for example, I would put myself down as a guy who pretty much had a good kick at the ball when I was competing. The marches were driven along and the strathspeys had a lift and drive. If someone had said that ABC were on the panel and they liked things softened down a bit, there is no way I would have done that."

John Wilson reckons that he could hold true to his principles when faced with a choice of playing the judges' way and winning a prize, or playing it his way and missing out on the prize list. "You have to ask what it is that is important. Is it only about being in the prize list? For some it might be and that's because it's such a big competitive world out there and the importance of building a track record is absolutely paramount to these individuals. In many ways that is what supports them for entry to the Northern Meetings and Argyllshire Gathering. But I wouldn't have changed, even if it took me out the prize list."

He is also a keen promoter of the variety that we are seeing in piping today, and the coming together of the pipes with many other traditional instruments. He is keen to see this development continue, with the great Highland bagpipe becoming more integrated into the mainstream traditional bands. "The issue is whether you consider what these bands are doing with traditional bagpipe music as disrespectful gauged against sitting back, taking a wider view, and asking if it's entertainment. 'Does it sound good musically?', as opposed to saying 'That's a really traditional march and they've changed the time signature and the rhythm and it's totally offensive to me.' There are people who will never move from that position, but there are also people who are open minded and who would embrace almost anything. They would argue that it's hard to disapprove because these bands are pulling in the crowds. Surely all of the people can't be wrong all of the time? I think we should embrace all who play the bagpipes and recognise that there will be extremes, but that happens in every art form. When I look at the opportunities for young people to come on board, the numbers that are actually playing, and the raw talent that I hear, you have to say that it's in a good state of health. Probably as good as it's ever been."

John Wilson on The Glenfiddich

As well as being a top class piper in his day John Wilson has another important ability - to be able to communicate with an audience without playing a note. It's not easy to stand up on a stage in front of hundreds of people and speak intelligently about a subject, even if you know it inside out. It's even less easy to know when to stop speaking and let the event continue. While there are those who say that John goes on for too long and they would rather listen to the music, what they often don't understand is that he only 'goes on' because the next competitor is not ready and without him saying anything there would be an empty stage and a restless audience.

John reckons that his most important task on the day is to ensure the players are kept calm, and nowhere is this more important than at Blair Castle for The Glenfiddich Championship where John regularly acts as Fear an Taighe. "My priority at The Glenfiddich is the competing pipers. Some of them just want to get out there as soon as the steward knocks on the door to tell them that the judges are ready for them. Others will take their time and make sure that they are happy that everything is together before they walk out of that tuning room. It is a bit stressful up there on the stage and I have to be conscious of the needs of the competing piper."

The word 'competing' is important on the day, and compèring a competition like The Glenfiddich is not the same as standing on stage at Celtic Connections, as John also does from time to time, to introduce pipers playing in recitals or in a concert setting. "I am conscious that The Glenfiddich competition isn't a concert and that the players are not going to start playing until they feel ready. There isn't that nice relaxed element that you have at a concert where you can take your time presenting someone, have them on stage with you, present them, and get the audience involved. It is a more formalised atmosphere at a competition. I need to be conscious of time and I need to make sure that I don't have any of the competitors telling me that I kept them waiting at the door for fifteen minutes while I prattled on."

On stage, John talks knowledgably about the tunes being played and it's obvious watching his performance that he has given his material a lot of thought, although as a competitor and judge at The Glenfiddich event in past years a lot of the material is very familiar. He takes a different approach to many who see their role as giving the audience a bit of history of each tune. "I don't break my back as far as the historical background is concerned because if you do look at the manuscript you'll see notes that say 'the tune is known as this, but is also known as that.'"

He cites as an example 'Isobel MacKay', which is a very graceful tune written about a beautiful and accomplished woman, but which is also referred to in some places by the title 'The Battle of Mulroy', which may have completely different connotations for some. So while Wilson is happy to let the audience have a feel for the provenance of a tune, especially if the composer is particularly significant, he is also keen to let the audience know what the player will be thinking about as they come on stage and the difficulties they may face.

It all sounds spontaneous when delivered to an appreciative audience but he has quite clearly done his homework. "Most of the information is already in my head, although I usually do have to sit until one in the morning the night before the competition since you don't have a lot of time between the pipers being given their tunes and the competition beginning. It's just a few words to say something about the tune and its attractions. It's about telling the audience that a particular tune is attractive or difficult because, for example, it is full of high G passages that are difficult to sustain and that might represent a major challenge to the piper. I might tell the audience that it is a tune that you have to create movement in or it will become monotonous. I have even been known to sing a bit of a tune to help the audience understand how the piper treats a variation to create, for example, a sense of ascendancy. It's all about giving the audience a bit more than 'It's about Lord so and so fighting for so and so at such and such a battle'."

It's a heavy day of music at Blair Castle for The Glenfiddich competition, with ten straight pìobaireachds, but the weight of the music is helped along by John's knowledgeable and entertaining introductions. It's appropriate that he treats his subject so seriously. Competitors and audience alike talk about The Glenfiddich in almost hushed reverential tones — the fact that what is officially known as 'The Glenfiddich Piping Championship' is universally shortened to 'The Glenfiddich' is testament to this. "I think what it may have done in the initial days was to generate a bit of careful playing because the stakes were high. In those days there were some big profile players who were well known for their individual style, 'grabbing a tune by the neck' and giving it a good shake. Some of these players, when they came to The Glenfiddich, adopted a more cautious approach thinking that if you are too flamboyant you might do something wrong."

"One of the major faults I pick up on in terms of adjudication, I call it a fault but it's really a comment, is the lack of contrast when presenting a pìobaireachd. The variations were not meant to all be played at the same pace. You need to inject shading into the presentation. There are tunes that are structured, like the 'Fingerlock' or 'The Vaunting', that are actually quite brutal pieces of music and you have to present them in a fairly brutal and curt manner. A short note is a short note and needs to be played as such. Someone who wants to play such tunes in a very cautious manner will actually just round off the sharp edges and soften the notational value of these notes and the delivery of these notes so it will be a safer presentation. There is a lot of that type of playing goes on nowadays and I feel a bit guilty about it because I get the impression from young players that they perceive that the senior judges have sent out this signal that it's all about keeping the tune correct technically. 'Don't be overzealous or over flamboyant in your style — play things down the middle, constant tempo and keep your pipes good during the presentation and you will be in the prize list' is what these adjudicators are saying, but if you want to go up there and really make a statement with your tune then some judges might take exception to your energy. As a result the obvious approach to winning prizes is just to take a very conservative middle line approach to your interpretation of the tunes."

John has been involved with the competition at Blair Castle almost since its inception in 1974 and speaks of the changes brought about since the competition was introduced in the early days. "When The Glenfiddich started I suppose one of the attractions was the money because they were offering money that no other competition could compete with. When I won the Gold Medal in 1968, for example, I won thirty-two pounds. I suppose that was a fair prize in those days but then The Glenfiddich came along and started paying appearance money to pipers so that we were guaranteed some remuneration for expenses before you had even kicked a ball."

John's footballing analogy is interesting because in a past era it could be argued footballers were more interested in winning games than in being paid for their work, and it raises the question as to whether this introduction of appearance money changed the way pipers approached the competition. "Before The Glenfiddich we just accepted that you went to competitions and if you didn't come into the prize list you had to cut your losses. I don't mean that to sound the wrong way but a lot of the focus from competing pipers when The Glenfiddich came along settled on the amount of money that was being offered by this new competition."

He is at pains to point out, however, that this concentration on reward was very short lived. "Over the years that has dissipated and now it's accepted that the big difference with The Glenfiddich is that, for just that one day of the year, it's just you and your peer group at the top level with the opportunity to share that big stage. Nowadays it's not about the money, even although it is significant and greater than ever before. I think other competitions offer substantial amounts of money as well, but The Glenfiddich has established itself now and I think it has reached the stage where it has a huge profile. It is up there with the Argyllshire Gathering and the Northern Meeting."

John Wilson believes that part of the reason for the success of The Glenfiddich competition, and the reason why so many of the contributors to this day enjoy it so much, lies with the sponsor. "You can't establish the profile and integrity of a competition overnight, no matter how much money you put into it — that's something that has developed over the years and I think the image of William Grant & Sons as a company has changed over the years as well, from being a big private concern going in with a dose of money, to nowadays being seen more as a benefactor to piping. Their commitment is fantastic. I don't see people like that as people who are in piping to get something out of it, rather I see them as the true mentors of piping in the old fashioned way — people who are totally focused in supporting piping for all of the right reasons."

Bob Worrall

Bob Worrall gives off an air of being at perfect peace with himself whether compering a major piping event or commentating on the World Championships for the BBC, but the reality is different. "You walk onto the stage at Glasgow Concert Hall with Field Marshal Montgomery just about to come on behind you, there are two and a half thousand people in the audience, and it's a who's who of piping. If people think for a second that I am at ease doing this then they're wrong."

Strangely, it was as a way of dealing with nerves that Bob started talking to audiences in the first place. "From the first time I did any sort of recital years ago, I felt I needed to talk to the audience and let them know a little about the tunes, tell a little anecdote or something. People would tell me afterwards how much they appreciated it but to be honest it's as much for me as it is for the audience. It allows me to get my wind back, control my nerves and establish a connection. Once you have that connection it's easier to strike up the pipes. If there's no connection that's when the nerves can take over. There's a selfish component to it as well. I love it as an audience member when someone does that. It's so much better than the player who comes out with a towel stuck in a sporran, looks at their notes, and plays without a word to the audience."

Little did Bob think that saying a few words before playing a tune at a recital would lead to a regular position as a commentator at the World Championships. "I got a call at home from one of the producers and he told me they were looking at covering the Worlds. They hadn't done it since the seventies, which I knew because I have copies of the programmes, which were great. They were going to have a chief commentator, Jackie Bird, and they needed an expert summariser or colour commentator and they wanted to know if I would be interested in doing it. I wasn't sure why my name should have been out there since I had no background in broadcasting. They seemed to know that already but they were looking for someone who could talk to an audience and who they could use in the programme to make commentary, someone who had judged the contest at some point in the past. I'd certainly done that bit, so I asked them to give me couple of weeks to talk about it at home."

Bob wasn't sure whether he should do it or indeed could do it. "I talked to a number of people over here and they all said, 'go for it', so when the producer called back I told him I was inclined to say yes but he would need to define the job. He couldn't do that since it was a brand new job, and said that I could get to define it myself. All he would say was that they were trying to haul in a general audience. They didn't want to alienate the people who wouldn't know what I was talking about if I was being too technical, but also didn't want to alienate the pipe band world either by saying 'Oh, here comes the so and so band in that lovely such and such tartan' and all that kind of cheesy stuff. I'd have to try to be a little more general, not too technical, in comments on performance so that I could educate the audience. I subsequently discovered they had gone to Ian Embleton at the RSPBA and asked if they could give the BBC a name from their panel who could do the job, and it was Ian who gave them my name."

BBC Scotland seem happy with the job that Bob is doing for them. "They keep asking for suggestions about how to do it differently but that their ratings are so good that they don't want to alter it too much. In an ideal world the programme would be longer and it would also be great if you had two people doing what I am doing — one in the booth and one running around the park with a roving microphone at the final tuning area. Imagine running up to Terry Tully and saying 'I see you're working on a couple of sets of pipes here. What's happening?' and Terry, in his own humble way, talking about certain chanters that were causing problems and certain players that would have to be dumped for the day. I know all these people, and you could do some really neat things with one in the booth and one running around hauling in friends that they know. We could do an awful lot with it but it would mean another camera team and it would be a tough thing to pull off."

Jackie Bird, Bob's 'chief commentator', and one of Scotland's best known broadcasters, is delighted he was chosen to be involved in the programme. "He made piping accessible to me. Sometimes people are so deeply entrenched in their subject that you get the impression that they don't want to share. Bob had none of that. It was a joy to find someone who wasn't only extraordinarily knowledgeable but such was his enthusiasm for the music that he was keen to share it with a comparative newcomer and showed never ending patience at explaining to me the nuances of piping. He really opened up the world of piping to me. And he is a joy to work with, that lovely smile and these crinkly eyes."

The Grade 1 event is streamed live on the internet and that gives thousands of pipe band enthusiasts from all over the world the opportunity to watch the most important event in the pipe band calendar. "The audience for the live streaming is huge. When I was in New Zealand recently I was talking to the Invercargill Pipe Band. They have several levels of bands and a band hall. Well, in New Zealand all the bands have band halls. They were all in their band hall with the wide screen TV and lap top, and it's not two or three people, it's dozens, or even hundreds. When BBC sees two or three hits it doesn't mean two or three people watching, it could be two or three hundred. There are huge band parties throughout Canada, the US and South Africa. I have friends in South Africa who are all in their band halls, fifty or more people watching in each hall, and they're making up t-shirts and having a real blast. For the bands that can't make it over every year for financial reasons it keeps them in the loop and keeps them connected."

It's a great role, and one that Bob obviously revels in, but it's not without its problems. "People keep pushing me to say controversial things and I don't know about that. I have to be guarded because it is live. While the band is playing I will write two or three notes down because they are looking for a comment in the live stream that they can use after the performance, which I don't talk over. They might take a comment and integrate it. After the band comes off and Jackie interviews the pipe major I might make a couple of comments before we go to the next band. In the lead up to the championship I will have been writing things down and listening to the medleys and MSRs that the bands will be playing and so I have a pretty good idea of what is coming in terms of tunes and everything else."

Bob's job is a serious one, and he's there to give professional commentary on the performance of the bands, but he also gets the opportunity to throw in some amusing anecdotes he has picked up on his travels. "There's a jig that Field Marshal Montgomery used to play, 'Sparky Cherry', which I found out came from one of the band's parties. It was initially an unnamed jig that Ryan Canning wrote and they were playing it after 'John Paterson's Mare'."

"At the party they were playing a game where you have to give the name of your first pet and your mother's maiden name and that is your porn star name. Richard Parkes was Sparky Cherry. I remember going into the booth getting ready, and they came in and asked if I had any questions. I asked if I could say the word 'porn' during the live stream, and Graham Mitchell, the director, told me that I couldn't, so I said that 'Sparky Cherry' was something to do with Richard Parkes's alter ego. The next day at the Piping Centre, Roddy MacLeod said 'I heard you yesterday, is that Richard Parkes' porn name?' Murray and Patricia Henderson were there with their daughters, and Patricia said to Faye, 'Tell Bob what your porn star name is'. She got all flustered and I said that I knew her mother's maiden name is Innes. It turns out the dog's name was Nipples because it kept having litter after litter of puppies, so Faye's name was Nipples Innes."

Bob loves getting little titbits like that for use on air, and also loves the fact that the programme is proving to be so popular. "I think they said last year that it was seen in eighty-four countries. That is just stunning."

It is stunning, to think that a programme on bagpipes has such a huge global audience. It has been a feather in the cap of the BBC, which for years was criticised for not providing adequate coverage of the World Pipe Band Championships. For Bob Worrall it's been a wee change from the judging he used to do on the third Saturday in August every year, and in fact, most other Saturdays as well. "By the time I stopped competing in the solo events I was pretty committed to my adjudicating work, and although the requests kept coming to take over bands, and play with bands, I kept saying no. Instead I became involved in our own Association by judging both solo competitions and bands. I was asked to help out with the certification system to certify adjudicators and put them through an examination process."

The process for certifying judges has become more complex over the years in order to ensure that bands and solo players are heard by as professionally qualified a panel of their peers as possible. "There are different levels of certificate for light music and pìobaireachd in the solo world, and for piping and ensemble adjudicators in the pipe band world, and I have been heavily involved in all of that. Other Associations in North America have come to us for help in developing a more professional adjudicators' certification programme, and we've been doing that. Helping them with certification and getting their first round of exams going and once it's in situ they have their own group of people who can administer it themselves."

There has been a huge movement of players across the world since Bob Worrall first visited Scotland in the mid-seventies, and the same thing is now happening with adjudicators. "The whole thing became global when our Association executive approached the RSPBA in the 1980s and asked about taking a look at some of our adjudicators becoming involved at the World Championships. They came back and said, 'show us your panel and their certification levels and show us what they've done'. We did that, and they recognised five people from our Association. It became a process where we made a nomination and if it was accepted then that person would go over and adjudicate. I was first put on at their request in

1987 and my first time judging was at Bellahouston Park in 1989. It just kind of went from there and the whole thing has become a bit different now with the international nature of adjudicators. It's all been broadened with a number of Australian and Canadian judges being recognised and utilised by the RSPBA. You can now go to a number of championships and you're likely to see non-UK based adjudicators. That's been happening in the last few years on the main solo benches as well."

Bob believes that all of the work that has been going on since the eighties is having a positive impact on the standard of adjudication across the board. "The overall background and depth of credentials that adjudicators have in the solo world, and I'm being careful how I put this one, is much better than existed thirty or forty years ago. With very few exceptions, the people you see adjudicating have been very successful performers in a competitive environment."

He believes that it is important that adjudicators are able to show these credentials. "I think you have to have done it. Maybe in the junior competitions it is easier to pick a winner and someone who doesn't have a strong competitive background may be able to adjudicate. When it gets to the high end the differences are so subtle, and they are stylistic. In many cases the minutiae that we are using to separate the quality of instruments and minor technical things that we're picking up on can't be noticed unless you have handled these issues yourself. The more skilled and the greater the depth of background of the adjudicator, the better the job they can do."

Plus there is the credibility factor. "That's the big one. I mean we have defined our own criteria of what we want someone to have done before we let them become adjudicators. That would include the number of years' experience and what kind of competitive experience, and that's there as much for credibility as for anything else. When a band goes to the line, or a solo player walks onto the platform, they want to look at the person with the clipboard and say 'excellent'. You don't want them going up to compete and look at the judges and say 'who's that?'"

There is certainly no question of anyone saying 'who is that?' when Bob Worrall walks onto a concert stage or takes his seat at a judges' table. He has had a hugely successful career and is one of the most recognised faces in the piping world. Now that he's had the luxury of being able to give up his day job, he is able to devote even more of his time to the world of piping. However, when you hear all of the things he did when he was working, you have to wonder where he ever had the time to play, compete or adjudicate. "I taught high school geography, firstly at Burlington and then Oakville, both in Ontario. I was also Department Head for the Social Science Programme. I coordinated student activities so as well as a full teaching load I had a heavy administration load. I would then come home and teach privately to piping pupils. I also had all the adjudication and weekend workshops, so life was becoming a bit of a chaotic whirlpool. When I hit the time that I could retire with an unreduced pension, I went. I still do a bit of substitute teaching now but the rest of it is just my piping and so my calendar is mine now"

His calendar might be his own these days, but it seems to be as full as ever. "This is my sixth year retired and it's so much easier. I've made a few trips to Australia, New Zealand and South Africa, and if I tried to do that before I retired I would manage one a year and have to request a leave of absence. Now I just go. There will be some times where two to three months in a row I am on the go every weekend, and I don't mean in Ontario. I will be on a flight somewhere, although it's usually broken up and it's not always the same thing. I had two weekends recently, one in Halifax and one in Chicago, and that was to help them with their ensemble certification for their judges. Prior to that it would be a teaching weekend. Then I did the BIG weekend for the Italian pipers with Roddy MacLeod and that was a teaching and playing weekend. I might do a band workshop and the band will want to have a concert at night and they might ask me to play a tune. That helps bring in a crowd and helps to offset their expenses."

Bob loves his music and is delighted to be able to spend his time in retirement helping others. This is partly because of the kindness that was shown to him when he first travelled to Scotland nearly forty years ago. Many of the players he met in those early trips impressed him, and not just because of their piping skills. "There were a number of people who caught my attention, and who were also really kind to me. They took me under their wing and made me feel part of it all, that I wasn't an outsider. Pipe Major Angus MacDonald without question was one of them. The first time I heard him play, when he took to the stage and struck up that bagpipe, it just about knocked me off my chair. He was really helpful to me and would give me little subtle bits of advice on the side, even although we were competing at the same events. John D Burgess was another one. Then there would be the likes of Hugh McCallum, John McDougall and Iain McFadyen. They were all hitting the boards at the time. I was younger than they were but they were all really good to me."

There were others who caught Bob's eye because of the impressive quality of their playing. "How could I forget the late Hugh McInnes playing marches. Absolutely stunning. You couldn't watch him because there were visual issues with the way he presented himself that were a bit strange, but if you closed your eyes it was like sitting back and listening to perfection. He was a superb march player."

"I can also remember one of the best jigs I ever heard. It was at the Skye Gathering Hall up in Portree and the late Willie MacDonald played the 'Tenpenny Bit'. The music was absolutely stunning. Without doubt it was the most musical jig I have ever heard. I never had a chance to hear much of Iain Morrison's playing, although I did compete against him when the Eagle Pipers had their invitational thing going back in the seventies. They invited ten or twelve players. I got invited twice and was second both times. The first time I was second to Iain Morrison who gave a stellar performance. He had an entirely different style, a refined march playing. What hit me was that all of his music had a lot of colour. I regret that I didn't have a chance to hear him play more. I did hear him playing in the Silver Chanter when he won it with 'The Lament for Mary MacLeod' and it was superb, first-rate playing."

"The second year at the Eagle Pipers, Donald MacPherson won it and that was a treat. I remember years later sitting on the judges' bench at the GS MacLennan Competition in San Diego with Donald and it was great, it was like turning full circle, sitting beside someone who you had competed against and who was one, or two, generations older, and then finally having a chance to adjudicate with them."

The one thing that all of the pipers and performances just mentioned have in common is musicality, and for Bob Worrall this is paramount, whether he is talking as a player or an adjudicator. "What is more important, music or technique? Music, no question. I have no problem with an early 'E' or a tiny late drone at the end of a performance. A little slip like that is no problem if the music is there. I think most of my judging colleagues would agree and are forgiving of the little things."

It's not just about forgiving the little mistakes for Bob, it's about taking a positive rather than a negative view of the role of an adjudicator. "If we didn't do that it would be negative judging and some people would call us the gracenote counters. They had an early 'E' so there is no way they could be in first place. Why not? Or this happened so they can't be in the prize list. Why not? It makes the judge's job too easy if we judge everything negatively. That being said, sometimes you're adjudicating a contest where many bands end up giving first rate musical performances. You are hoping for a barnstormer of a performance which will make your job easy. But, in the end, with several very strong performances, you end up having to balance out and take into consideration all the small things that took away from perfection."

The other thing that makes the judge's job difficult is that there are just so many top class players, both solo and in bands, these days. "The piping scene is very healthy. For young kids coming along now it's great. When I was young you kept it quiet if you were studying bagpipes since it was a kind of nerdy thing to do. Not today. It's cool and the kids who study it are revered. Of course technology has helped. Every week I have lessons with people who live in isolated spots via Skype. We can sort out problems over Skype and catch up with news. People don't have to wonder how Shotts is playing under Ryan Canning or whatever because we are all so connected. David Wilton had pictures up from The Glenfiddich last year as it happened, and the live streaming was going. Colin MacLellan, Jenny Hazzard, Michael Grey and I were watching it from a vineyard in Italy. And it was good wine! A healthy state of affairs indeed."

Appendix: A Guide To Competition Piping, by James Beaton

Since the end of the 18th century, much of the focus in professional and indeed amateur piping has been on playing the bagpipes in competition, and as a consequence competition piping is a major theme of A Piper's Tale. The first formal solo piping competition took place in 1781 at the Falkirk Tryst, where many Highlanders gathered after driving their cattle to the Lowlands for sale. The descendants of this competition are now run throughout Scotland and overseas, via piping associations as well as Highland Games. Competition is also important in the pipe band world, with the first formal pipe band competition taking place at Cowal Highland Gathering in 1906.

It is important to look at how piping competitions are organised today, and what are the various important ones which feature in this book, both from the point of view of solo playing and pipe bands.

Turning first to solo playing, the Highland games circuit which is a feature of life in Scotland throughout the summer is of huge importance. At each of these games there is usually a competition for adults and under-18s in both light music and pìobaireachd.

Light music comprises marches in 2/4 time, strathspeys in 4/4 time and reels in 2/2 time, the latter two categories of tunes being descended from Gaelic mouth music and dance tunes. Pìobaireachd is descended from Gaelic song and harp music, and is much more complex than light music, the pieces comprising a theme and increasingly technically complex variations.

The adult competitions are graded by the Competing Pipers' Association (a membership body which represents the views of pipers involved in adult competition), into C, B, A and Premier grades, in growing order of ability and achievement for both light music and pìobaireachd.

Progression from a lower grade to a higher grade is dependent on ability and competing success.

Premier grade players are players who have won one of the most highly regarded competitions, which are the Gold Medals for pìobaireachd, or have won the light music competitions at the Argyllshire Gathering in Oban or the Northern Meeting in Inverness.

The Argyllshire Gathering and the Northern Meeting are the

two most important piping competitions on the circuit. Individuals who win at these are considered to have reached the pinnacle of their piping careers.

Winning the Gold Medal for pìobaireachd at either entitles the winner to go on and play in the Senior Pìobaireachd at Oban or the Clasp to the Gold Medal at Inverness.

Once a player has won one of the Gold Medals, he or she can no longer compete in that competition. The same system applies for light music competitions at these games. Winning either the March, or the Strathspey and Reel competition means that the player progresses to the Former Winners' March, Strathspey and Reel, a test of technical and musical ability. At the Argyllshire Gathering, the player has to submit six marches, six strathspeys and six reels, from which one of each category is chosen, with each tune being played twice over. The same number of tunes must be submitted for this competition at the Northern Meeting, with two of each being chosen for the competitor to be played in turn.

The Glenfiddich competition is held annually at Blair Castle in Perthshire each year. It is regarded as the pinnacle of the solo competing world, and participants (of whom there are ten) qualify by winning the following competitions:

X   The previous year's Glenfiddich Championship

X   The Clasp at the Northern Meeting

X   The Senior Pìobaireachd at the Argyllshire Gathering

X   The Silver Star Former Winners March, Strathspey and Reel at the Argyllshire Gathering

X   The Silver Star Former Winners March, Strathspey and Reel at the Northern Meeting

X   The Bratach Gorm at the Scottish Piping Society of London's competition

X   The Gold Medal for Pìobaireachd at the Argyllshire Gathering

X   The Gold Medal for Pìobaireachd at the Northern Meeting

X   The Overall Prize at the Scottish Piping Society of

London's competition

X   The Winner of the Masters Invitational at the Glasgow International Piping Festival, Piping Live!

Pipe band competitions occur worldwide, but the most important one is the World Pipe Band Championships which occur in August every year, currently held at Glasgow Green in Glasgow, and is organised by the Royal Scottish Pipe Band Association.

The pipe band world is also divided into grades and at the top are the 33 or so bands who comprise Grade 1 and compete at the top level. As many of the bands are from overseas, in particular from Australia, New Zealand, the United States and Canada, not all of the bands compete in the Championships every year, and the competition usually consists of some 17 bands after a qualification heat for the non-seeded bands. In the final, each band is asked to play twice. Firstly a march, strathspey and reel set, chosen from one of two submitted, and then a medley, again usually one chosen from two submitted, which is a more free form selection of music lasting between five and seven minutes. Pipe bands are judged on the quality of piping, the quality of drumming and the quality of ensemble play.

Acknowledgements

There are a lot of people whose help has been invaluable, and without whom this project would never have left the tuning room. All of the pipers involved have given their valuable time to talk to me, and then to make sure that the words I ascribed to them were accurate, and reflected the tales they wanted to tell. They have all been refreshingly open in their conversations, giving not only of their time but also of their opinions and hopefully a little bit of the psychology that has made them so successful in the field of piping in which they have chosen to play.

Dr. Alistair Braidwood has done a sterling job editing my words. It wasn't easy for him, coming from a non-piping background, and his early communications to me were littered with questions like 'Why do they keep talking about the ground?', 'What's a tarlouth?' and 'Is Kenmure's Up And Awa' Willie one tune or two?'

James Beaton at the National Piping Centre has read every word of my original manuscript and ensured that I knew that Roddy is a Mac but Willie is a Mc. He has checked the spelling of the tunes and the competitions. His closing piece on the working of the competition world will prove useful for non-competing pipers and non-pipers alike.

William Grant & Sons have provided valuable support that has helped me take the time needed to pull all of this together and for that, as well as their continuing role supporting all manner of piping events, I thank them. Their help also means that a portion of any profits from this book can go to the Friends of Plockton Music School to help with the work done with a really talented bunch of students at the National Centre for Excellence in Traditional Music.

Derek Maxwell has been photographing piping events for years and I am grateful to him for the access he gave to his valuable library of photographs for inclusion in the book.

I first met Carlos Nuñez in Ortigueira about ten years ago when I went to the Festival there with the National Youth Pipe Band of Scotland when Paul Warren was unable to make it. We have met, and played together, on many occasions since and his professionalism and enthusiasm never cease to amaze me. His thoughtful and considered Foreword to the book is a most useful addition.

Eddi Reader is one of our best-loved singers, a superb interpreter of the works of Robert Burns and a regular at the His

Nibs sessions mentioned in my introduction. Her reflections on the pipes and her family are fascinating and I look forward to reading the book she is currently researching on that history.

I mentioned Hugh Wilson and Cumbernauld Caledonia Pipe Band. There were so many there in the early days that helped nurture my enthusiasm for the music. Ken Roberts, Andy Arbuckle, Eric Craddock, Jimmy Kinloch, and Ronnie Hambley were all instrumental in helping me learn and improve. As with many others mentioned in these pages, they all did it for nothing. No money ever changed hands. They, and hundreds of others up and down the country, and in fact right across the world, were, and continue to be, enthusiastic amateurs. Their infectious energy encourages generation after generation to pick up and play bagpipes.

The man who helped me more than most, sadly no longer with us, was my Dad John. He used to drive me to practice several times a week. Initially he sat in his car during the band practice at Seafar School. Then he came in and listened. The next thing I knew he was the Band Treasurer and he was spending his weekends coming to competitions with us as well. Without support from him and my mum I wouldn't be sitting here writing this now.

Finally, Jane and Max, my wife and son. I love them both and I admire, and thank them for, their patience over the last twelve months as I disappeared yet again to listen, write and edit.